CLB 1638
© 1987 Colour Library Books Ltd., Godalming, Surrey, England
All rights reserved
This edition published in 1993 by SMITHMARK Publishers Inc.,
16 East 32nd Street, New York, NY 10016
SMITHMARK books are available for bulk purchase for sales promotion
and premium use. For details write or call the manager of special sales,
SMITHMARK Publishers Inc., 16 East 32nd Street,
New York, NY 10016; (212) 532-6600.
ISBN 0-8317-9113-6
Printed in Singapore

Text by
Lalita Ahmed
Photography by
Peter Barry
Designed by
Philip Clucas

VEGETARIAN
COOKING

SMITHMARK

Mixed Vegetable Raita (top), Noodles
(below left) and New Potato Fry (bottom
right).

Contents

Introduction
page 7

Salads
pages 22-26

Soups
pages 8-12

Rice and Pulses
pages 27-29

Snacks and Appetizers
pages 13-21

Bread and Pizza
pages 30-35

Main Meals
pages 36-49

Sauces, Dips and Chutneys
pages 50-55

Sweets
pages 56-63

Index
page 64

This page: Greenbeans with Coconut (top) and Spinach with Paneer (above). Facing page: Vegetable Stir Fry.

Introduction

It is amazing how rigid we are when it comes to the subject of food and what we eat. In all other aspects of life virtually anything goes: people walk the streets with pink hair; sail the Atlantic single-handed or jog around the houses for two hours every morning and yet if we prefer beans and lentils to beef and chicken we are considered as being rather odd.

Vegetarians are not cranks, and there is nothing weird and wonderful about a pattern of vegetarian eating; they just prefer to eat dishes which do not contain meat, poultry, game and, quite often, fish. 'Why don't they become ill?' you hear people say; 'Where do they get their energy from if they don't eat meat?'; 'How boring to live on just vegetables and those little dried peas!' As vegetarians will happily tell you, they feel perfectly healthy, have quite sufficient energy to cope with day-to-day activities and, above all, *they really enjoy their food.*

A vegetarian diet can be just as varied and interesting as one based on meat and fish. Meat is much the same the world over, which cannot be said of the wide and wonderful range of fresh fruits and vegetables. And it is variety which is very much the keynote of vegetarian eating: different pastas, rices, cheeses, nuts and pulses are just a selection of the varied ingredients of a vegetarian diet. Most important of all, vegetarian dishes are every bit as nutritious as their meat-rich counterparts. The main difference lies with the types of food which provide us with the necessary nutrients. In a typical vegetarian dish, the protein usually comes from pulses, nuts or cheese, or a combination of these ingredients. Minerals, vitamins, fats and carbohydrates come from all the other basic foods, such as those already mentioned.

Eating 'the vegetarian way' has all sorts of advantages in its favor. A meatless diet is a very healthy one since it is nutritious, low in fat and high in bulk and fiber. Vegetarians rarely need to watch their weight as a diet that is high in natural fiber and low in fat is comparatively low in calories. The traditional pattern of Western eating is relatively expensive to follow, whereas vegetarian dishes are more economical to prepare and cook. In fact, meatless meals can simply make a nice change from the traditional pattern of eating. Vegetarian cooking is fun, and eating vegetarian meals is healthy and good for you.

Vegetarian food really can be exciting and delicious and even if you are not a committed vegetarian many of the ideas in this section are well worth trying. The dishes combine unusual tastes and textures with an imaginative use of spices and fresh herbs for extra flavor. If you served many of the recipes to your family and friends they probably wouldn't even realize that their meal was meatless.

Soups

Cucumber Soup

PREPARATION TIME: 15 minutes

COOKING TIME: 8-10 minutes

SERVES: 4 people

1 large cucumber
1 cup water
2½ cups vegetable stock
1¼ tblsp white wine vinegar
2½ tblsp cornstarch mixed with
2½ tblsp water
2½ tblsp soured cream
2½ tblsp natural yogurt
Salt and ground white pepper to taste
1¼ tblsp chopped chives or scallion tops
Chili powder

Cut ¼ of the cucumber into wafer thin rounds and keep aside for garnishing. Puree the rest of the cucumber with the water in a liquidizer. Put the vegetable stock and the pureed cucumber into a saucepan and bring to the boil over a medium heat. Add the vinegar and cook for 1 minute. Add the cornstarch mixture gradually. Stir well until the soup starts to thicken. Simmer for 2-3 minutes. Remove from the heat and cool slightly. Blend in the liquidizer and add the soured cream and yogurt. Return to the saucepan and season with salt and pepper. Heat through gently to serve hot or chill to serve cold. Serve garnished with sliced cucumber and chopped chives or scallion tops. Dust with chili powder.

Daal Soup

This is a thick and hearty soup, made from lentils. The lentils most often used for making soup are red lentils, or yellow lentils which are called Toor daal. The recipe below can be made with either variety.

PREPARATION TIME: 15-20 minutes

COOKING TIME: 15 minutes

SERVES: 4-6 people

3 cups red lentils (see above)
3¾ cups water
4 canned tomatoes, drained and crushed

1 green chili, sliced lengthways and seeded
2½ tblsp natural yogurt or soured cream
1 tblsp butter
1 medium onion, peeled and chopped
Salt and freshly ground black pepper to taste
1-2 sprigs fresh green coriander leaves, chopped

Wash the lentils in 4-5 changes of water. Drain the lentils and put them into a pan with the water. Cover the pan and bring to the boil; simmer for 10 minutes. Beat until smooth with an egg whisk. Add the crushed tomatoes and green chili and simmer gently for 2 minutes. Stir in the yogurt or soured cream. Melt the butter in a small pan and fry the onion until golden. Season the hot soup with salt and pepper and pour into a serving bowl; sprinkle with the fried onion and chopped coriander. Serve immediately with buttered brown bread, crisp rolls or croutons.

Tomato Saar

This is a thin tomato soup from the South of India. It makes a refreshing and interesting starter.

PREPARATION TIME: 15 minutes

COOKING TIME: 17-18 minutes

SERVES: 4-6 people

2½ tsp butter
1 small onion, peeled and chopped
½lb tomatoes, skinned and chopped
4 cups water
1¼ tblsp tomato paste
4-6 green Cilantro (Chinese Parsley) leaves
Salt and freshly ground black pepper to taste
3 cloves of garlic, peeled and crushed

Garnish
1-2 sprigs fresh green coriander or parsley leaves, chopped
1 green chili, chopped (optional)

Melt half of the butter and fry the onion for 3-4 minutes. Add the skinned and chopped tomatoes and cook for 5 minutes. Blend the

water and tomato paste and add to the onion and tomatoes. Add Cilantro (Chinese Parsley) leaves. Season with salt and pepper. Cover and simmer for 5-7 minutes. Heat the remaining butter and fry the crushed cloves of garlic until dark brown. Pour the mixture over the simmering tomato soup. Remove from the heat. Sprinkle over the chopped coriander and chili. Discard green chili before eating. Serve piping hot either with French bread or with a little plain boiled rice. Alternatively: blend the skinned tomatoes to give a smooth textured soup.

Mixed Vegetable Soup

This Indian recipe can include a wide variety of vegetables. One creates one's own dish by adding or subtracting one or more vegetables.

PREPARATION TIME: 15 minutes

COOKING TIME: about 20 minutes

SERVES: 6 people

2½ tsp butter
1 medium onion, peeled and chopped
6 cloves
1 inch piece cinnamon stick
4 small green cardamoms
1 small bayleaf
1 medium potato, peeled and chopped
2 carrots, peeled and chopped
1 banana, peeled and chopped
6 flowerets of cauliflower
½ cup shelled fresh or frozen peas
1 leek, washed and chopped
1 stick celery, chopped
½ cup green beans (sliced or chopped)
4 cups water
Salt and freshly ground black pepper to taste

Garnish
1-2 sprigs fresh green coriander
1-2 green chilies chopped

Melt the butter in a large saucepan and fry the onion for 3 minutes. Add the cloves, cinnamon, cardamom, bayleaf and fry for 1 minute. Add the potato, carrots, banana and cauliflower. Fry for 3 minutes. Add the remaining vegetables and cook for 2-3 minutes. Add water and salt and

pepper to taste. Cover and sim gently for 8-13 minutes until vegetables are cooked. Adjust seasoning. Garnish with choppe coriander leaves and green chil Discard green chilies before eat The vegetables should float in t clear soup; do not blend.

Carrot Soup

PREPARATION TIME: 12 minu

COOKING TIME: 20-25 minut

SERVES: 4 people

4-6 carrots, peeled and cut into t slices
1 medium onion, peeled and quartered
1 medium turnip, peeled and cut wedges
2 cloves garlic, peeled
3 cups water or vegetable stock
¾ tsp dried thyme
Salt and ground white pepper to
Hot pepper sauce to taste

Garnish
1 tblsp toasted sunflower seeds, flaked almonds and pistachio (mixed together)

Put the carrots, onion, turnip, g and water into a large saucepan Cover and simmer for 15 minu Add thyme and salt and peppe taste and simmer for a further minutes. Cool slightly and blen a liquidizer. Return to the sauce and heat the soup through. Lad the soup into bowls. Add hot pepper sauce to taste. Serve garnished with toasted nuts.

Facing page: Tomato Saar (
right), Daal Soup (center le
and Mixed Vegetable Soup
(bottom).

Minestrone Soup

This famous vegetable and pasta soup from Italy can be made in many different ways. The recipe below is a simple, but delicious one – served with bread, it is a complete meal in itself.

PREPARATION TIME: 20 minutes
COOKING TIME: 30 minutes
SERVES: 4-6 people

4 tblsp olive oil
1 medium onion, peeled and chopped
2 cloves of garlic, peeled and crushed
2 medium potatoes, peeled and diced
3 carrots, peeled and diced
2 stalks celery, chopped
1½ cups shredded cabbage
4-5 skinned or canned tomatoes, chopped
3¾ cups water or vegetable stock
1 bouquet garni
1½ cups shelled fresh, or frozen peas

Quick Tomato Soup (above right), Minestrone Soup (right) and Onion Soup (far right).

cup boiled and cooked red kidney
beans
up macaroni or any shaped pasta
lt and freshly ground black pepper
to taste
cup grated Parmesan cheese

eat the olive oil in a saucepan and
the onion and garlic until the
ion is soft, 2-3 minutes. Stir in

the potatoes, carrots and celery
and fry for 3 minutes; add the
cabbage and tomatoes. Cook for 5-
6 minutes. Add water or stock and
bouquet garni. Add peas, kidney
beans, pasta and simmer gently,
covered, for 10-15 minutes, or until
the pasta is just tender. Season
with salt and pepper and ladle into

bowls. Sprinkle generously with
grated Parmesan cheese before
serving. Serve Minestrone soup
with crusty bread.

Quick Tomato Soup

This is quite an exotic soup and is
made within a few minutes. It is
ideal for a hot summer's day.

PREPARATION TIME: 10 minutes
plus chilling time

SERVES: 4-6 people

2½ cups chilled tomato juice
¼ cup fresh or canned tomato paste,
   chilled
¾ tsp hot red pepper sauce
¾ tsp grated lemon peel
¾ tsp grated orange peel
¼-⅓ cup dry white wine
Salt and ground white pepper to taste
Little iced water
4 tblsp natural yogurt
⅓ cup soured cream
6 balls of honeydew melon
6 balls of water melon
6 balls of ripe pear

Garnish
Mint leaves

Mix the tomato juice, tomato
paste, pepper sauce, fruit peels and
wine together. Season with salt and
pepper, cover and refrigerate for 3-
4 hours. Thin the soup with a little
iced water if necessary. Whisk the
yogurt and cream together until
smooth and light. Divide the soup
amongst 4-6 bowls. Spoon the
yogurt and cream mixture into the
centre of each portion and float the
fruit balls on top. Garnish with
mint leaves and serve.

Rice and Mushroom Soup

Ideal for a party or for summer afternoons.

PREPARATION TIME: 10 minutes

COOKING TIME: 40-50 minutes

SERVES: 6-8 people

1 cup wild rice or brown rice
1 cup water
2 tblsp butter
1 medium onion, peeled and finely
    chopped
1 stalk celery, chopped
1 cup mushrooms, chopped
1 level tsp powdered garam masala
    (hot aromatic powder)
1 level tsp ground mustard seed
Salt and freshly ground black pepper
    to taste
4 cups water or stock
2 tblsp cornstarch blended with
2½ tblsp water
⅓ cup light cream

Garnish
1-2 sprigs fresh green coriander or
    parsley, chopped

Wash the rice in 3-4 changes of water; cook covered in 1 cup water for 25-30 minutes, or until rice is tender. Keep on one side. Melt the butter in a large saucepan; saute the onion until tender for 3-5 minutes. Add the celery and mushrooms. Cook for 1-2 minutes. Stir in the powdered garam masala, mustard and salt and pepper to taste. Add the water or stock. Simmer for 5 minutes. Add the cornstarch mixture and simmer for a further 3 minutes. Add the cooked rice and cream. Gently stir over a low heat for 2 minutes to heat through. Ladle the soup into bowls and garnish with coriander or parsley.

Onion Soup

Onion soup has been made famous by the French. Here is a delicious recipe based on the French style.

PREPARATION TIME: 20 minutes

COOKING TIME: 1 hour

SERVES: 4-6 people

6 tblsp butter
3-4 large onions, peeled and sliced
    into rings
2½ tblsp flour
3¾ cups vegetable stock
Salt and ground white pepper to taste
6 slices of French bread (¾ inch)
    thick
2 cloves of garlic, peeled and bruised
6 tblsp grated Parmesan cheese

Melt the butter in a saucepan and fry the onions briskly on a very low heat. Cover and simmer the onions in their own juices for 25-30 minutes, stirring occasionally until golden brown. Remove from the heat. Stir in the flour and add the stock gradually. Season with salt and pepper and return to heat. Bring to the boil quickly; reduce the heat and simmer covered for 15-20 minutes. Rub the bread pieces each side with the bruised garlic. Float the bread rounds in the soup and sprinkle grated Parmesan cheese generously over the top. Put under the broiler and cook for 2-3 minutes or until the top is golden. Serve at once. Alternatively – fry the bread rounds or bread slices in butter prior to rubbing with garlic.

Carrot Soup (top), Rice and Mushroom Soup (center ri[g]) and Cucumber Soup (botto[m] left).

Snacks and Appetizers

...lour Pancake

...his is a favorite pancake from the ...uthern part of India and it is ...ally worth making; good, ...holesome and nutritious.

...REPARATION TIME: 10 minutes
...OOKING TIME: 20 minutes
...RVES: 6 people

...2 cups whole-wheat flour
...tsp salt
...cup natural yogurt
...gg, beaten
...mall onion, peeled and chopped
...2 green chilies, chopped
...prigs fresh green coriander leaves,
...chopped
...tblsp grated fresh coconut, or
...desiccated coconut
...2 tsp sugar
...live oil

...eve the flour and salt and add the ...gurt and egg. Mix in sufficient ...ater to make a thickish batter of ...ouring consistency. Beat the ...xture well and add the onion, ...ili, coriander, coconut and sugar. ...ix well. Allow to stand for 2-3 ...nutes. Heat 1¼ tblsp oil in a ...all frying pan or omelette pan. ...oon in a little of the batter to ...ve a depth of 1¼ inches. Cover ...th a lid and cook over a low heat ...r 3-5 minutes. Turn the pancake ...er and pour a little oil around the ...ge; cover and cook until the ...ncake is set and brown on both ...les. Repeat with the remaining ...tter until you have several ...ncakes. Serve piping hot.

...osas

...osas can be eaten plain or with a ...ing. Eat them as a snack, for ...eakfast, or as a main meal with a ...ing and accompanied by chutney ...d daal (lentil dish).

...EPARATION TIME: overnight,
...us 20 minutes
...OOKING TIME: 30-45 minutes
...RVES: 6 people

...rice
...b white lentils (urid daal)
...tsp fenugreek seeds

1¼ tsp dried yeast
1¼ tsp sugar
¾ tsp salt
1¼ tblsp natural yogurt
Olive oil

Wash the rice and white lentils separately in 3-4 changes of water. Soak in fresh water for 1 hour. Grind the rice with a little water to a thick, coarse paste. Grind the white lentils with fenugreek seeds and a little water into a fine paste. (Use a food processor, food liquidizer or food grinder). Mix the dried yeast with 1¼ tblsp tepid water and the sugar. Mix well and leave to stand for 10 minutes until frothy. Mix the ground rice and lentils with the salt, yeast and yogurt and mix well. Cover with a cloth and leave in a dark, warm place overnight. Next day mix well with sufficient water to give a smooth, thickish batter. Heat a medium non-stick frying pan and grease well with 1¼ tsp oil. Pour in 2½-3¾ tblsp of the rice batter,

Bessan Omelette (top right), Flour Pancake (center left) and Dosas (bottom).

spread it around to make a thin pancake. Cover with a lid. Cook for 3-4 minutes; spoon a little oil around the edge of the frying pan and turn the dosa over. Cook for a

further 2-3 minutes and serve hot. make the remaining dosa in the same way. Dosas can be made as large as 12-14 inches in diameter.

Vegetable Filling

4 tblsp olive oil
2 large onions, peeled and thinly sliced
1¼ tsp white lentils (urid daal), washed and soaked in water for 5-10 minutes
½ tsp mustard seed
8-10 fresh Chinese parsley leaves
2 green chilies, cut into quarters
1½lb potatoes, boiled in their skins, peeled and cubed
Salt to taste

Heat oil and fry the onions for 4-5 minutes or until light brown. Add the drained lentils and mustard seed. Fry for ½ minute; add the curry leaves and green chilies. Add the potatoes and salt to taste. Cover and cook for 8-10 minutes, stirring occasionally. To serve: make the dosa as above and place 2½ tblsp of the potato filling in the centre; fold the dosa over like an omelette.

Samosa

These crispy triangles with a vegetable filling can be eaten hot or cold.

| **PREPARATION TIME:** 40 minutes |
| **COOKING TIME:** 25 minutes |
| **SERVES:** 4-6 people |

Pastry

2½ cups all purpose flour, sieved
½ tsp salt
½ tsp baking powder
Water

Make the dough by adding water, a little at a time, to the sieved flour, salt and baking powder. Mix to a soft pliable dough. Cover and allow to stand.

Filling

¼ cup oil
1 medium onion, peeled and chopped
4 cups potatoes, peeled and cubed
2 carrots, peeled and grated
½ cup shelled green peas
½ cup green beans, chopped
1¼ tsp chili powder
1¼ tsp salt
1¼ tsp garam masala powder (hot aromatic powder)
¾ tsp ground turmeric
1¼ tblsp dry mango powder, or lemon juice
Oil for deep frying

Heat the oil and fry the onions for 2-3 minutes. Add the potatoes and carrots and cook for 3 minutes. Add peas and beans and cook for 2-3 minutes. Sprinkle chili, salt, garam masala, turmeric and mango powder. Mix well, cover and cook till potatoes are tender. Remove from heat and allow to cool. Divide the dough into 12-14 equal sized balls; roll each one out on a floured surface to a thin circle, 2-3 inches in diameter. Cut each circle in half. Apply the flour paste on the straight edge of each half. bring the edges together, overlapping them so as to make a cone. Fill the cone with the filling. Apply a little flour paste on the open edge and seal by pressing both the edges together. This will make a triangular shape.

Make all the samosas in the same way. Heat the oil for deep frying. When the oil is hot, reduce the heat and fry the samosas, a few at a time, until golden brown on either side (about 4-5 minutes). Drain on kitchen paper and serve with chutney or tomato sauce.

Curry Puffs

Like sausage rolls, curried vegetable puffs make an ideal dish for snacks and cocktails. The size can be varied to suit the occasion.

| **PREPARATION TIME:** 1 hour |
| **COOKING TIME:** 20 minutes |
| **SERVES:** 4-6 |

1lb ready-made puff pastry

Filling

¼ cup oil
1 large onion, peeled and chopped
1¼ tsp cumin seeds
4 cups potatoes, peeled and diced
2 carrots, peeled and shredded
1 cup shelled peas
1¼ tsp salt
1¼ tsp freshly ground black pepper
2-3 sprigs fresh green coriander leaves, chopped
1¼ tsp garam masala powder (hot aromatic powder)

Flour paste: mix together 2½ tsp flour with water to make a sticky paste.

Heat the oil and fry the onion for 2 minutes. Add cumin seeds and allow to crackle, then add the diced potatoes. Stir fry over a medium heat for 5-6 minutes. Add the carrots and stir fry for 2 minutes. Add the peas and season with salt, pepper and chopped coriander leaves. Stir well. Cover and cook for 5-6 minutes or until the potatoes are tender. Sprinkle with the garam masala and lemon juice. Mix well. Remove from the heat and allow to cool. Roll out the puff pastry thinly. Cut into 3 inch by 6 inch rectangles. Place 1¼ tblsp filling at one end and roll up the pastry like jelly roll. Secure the ends with the flour and water paste. Preheat the oven to 375°F.

Potato Cutlets (top), Samosa (above left) and Curry Puffs (left).

Arrange the curry puffs on greased cooky sheets and bake for 10-15 minutes or until golden. Serve hot with tomato sauce.

Potato Cutlets

PREPARATION TIME: 30 minutes

COOKING TIME: 30 minutes

SERVES: 6 people

1¼ tblsp oil
1 medium onion, peeled and chopped
1½ cups shelled peas
6 cups potatoes, boiled in their skins, peeled and mashed
1¼ tsp salt
1¼ tsp freshly ground black pepper
2½ tblsp lemon juice
2 eggs, beaten
Breadcrumbs
Oil for shallow frying

Heat 1¼ tblsp oil in a frying pan and fry the onion for 3 minutes; add the peas and fry for 2 minutes. Mix the onion and peas with the mashed potatoes. Add salt and pepper to taste and the lemon juice. Mix well. Divide mixture into 24-30 small even-sized cakes. Dip firstly into beaten egg and then coat evenly with breadcrumbs. Heat sufficient oil in a frying pan for shallow frying. Shallow fry the potato cutlets for 3-4 minutes or until golden. Serve hot or cold with chutney or tomato sauce.

Bessan Omelettes

These vegetarian omelettes are made with chickpea (baisen) flour and can be eaten as a quick snack. Easy to make and quick to prepare, they are ideal for unexpected friends or late night guests.

PREPARATION TIME: 10 minutes

COOKING TIME: 20 minutes

MAKES: 12

2½ cups sieved bessan flour (made from chick-peas)
1 small onion, peeled and finely chopped
1-2 green chilies, chopped (optional)
2 sprigs fresh green coriander, chopped
2 tomatoes, seeded and diced
½ cup shelled peas
¾ tsp salt
Pinch chili powder
Olive oil

Mix the bessan flour with the onion, chilies, coriander, tomatoes and peas. Add sufficient water to made a thick batter, about 1¾ cups. Season with salt and chili powder, Mix well and allow to stand for 5 minutes. Heat a solid based frying pan or griddle pan and brush with oil. Ladle in sufficient batter to cover the base of the pan. Cover and cook over a low heat for 4-5 minutes. Turn the omelette over and cook for 3-4 minutes. Both sides should be browned evenly. Make the rest of the omelettes in the same way. Serve hot with tomato sauce.

Stuffed Summer Squash

Summer Squash can be stuffed with a vegetable or meat filling. Here is a delectable recipe for a vegetable stuffed Summer Squash.

PREPARATION TIME: 15 minutes

COOKING TIME: 45 minutes

SERVES: 4-6 people

2 Summer Squash 6-8 inches in length

Filling
¼ cup oil
1 large onion, peeled and chopped
4 cups potatoes, peeled and diced
1¼ tsp crushed fresh root ginger
1¼ tsp crushed garlic
1¼ tsp chili powder
¾ tsp turmeric powder
1¼ tsp garam masala powder (hot aromatic powder)

1 cup shelled peas
4 tomatoes, chopped
¾ tsp salt
¾ tsp freshly ground black pepper
1 green chili, chopped
2½ tsp melted butter

Heat the oil in a wok or large frying pan and fry the onion for 2 minutes. Add the potatoes and stir-fry for 3-4 minutes. Add the ginger, garlic, chili powder, turmeric and garam masala powder. Mix well and add the peas, tomatoes, salt and pepper and the green chili; cover and cook until the potatoes are tender, about 6-8 minutes. Add the lemon juice. Remove a thin slice from each end of the summer squash. Scoop out the centre pith leaving a ¾ inch shell. Remove the skin in alternate strips to give it firmness. Fill the hollowed summer squash with the prepared potato filling. Place the stuffed summer

squash on a rectangle of foil and brush with melted butter; season with salt and pepper. Wrap the foil around the summer squash; bake at 350°F for 40-45 minutes. Remove the foil from time to time and brush with the juices. Serve hot.

Vegetable Kebabs

This Turkish/Greek recipe makes an ideal side dish for barbecue parties.

PREPARATION TIME: 30 minutes

COOKING TIME: 30 minutes

SERVES: 4-6 people

1 eggplant cut into 1 inch pieces
1 large green pepper, seeded and cut into 1 inch pieces
12-14 small cherry tomatoes (or 6-8 tomatoes, halved)
12-14 small onions, peeled and blanched for 5 minutes
12-14 large mushrooms
2 medium potatoes, boiled in their skins, peeled and cut into 1 inch cubes
Olive oil
2½ tblsp lemon juice
½ tsp salt
¾ tsp freshly ground black pepper

Put all the vegetables into a large bowl and add 60ml (4 tblsp) olive oil, lemon juice and salt and pepper. Mix together and leave to stand for 10-15 minutes, turning the vegetables once or twice. Thread the vegetables alternately onto skewers. Brush with the marinade. Broil for 3-4 minutes, until evenly browned. Brush the vegetables with oil or marinade during grilling. Serve piping hot.

Stuffed Peppers

PREPARATION TIME: 30 minutes

COOKING TIME: 30-40 minutes

SERVES: 6 people

6 even sized peppers (green or red)
¼ cup oil
1 medium onion, peeled and chopped
2 cloves garlic, peeled and chopped
2 tomatoes, chopped
1 green chili, chopped
1 cup plain boiled rice
1 medium potato, peeled and diced
½ tsp salt

¾ tsp freshly ground black pepper
½ cup shelled peas
1¼ tblsp lemon juice
1¼ tblsp chopped parsley or cor leaves
2½ tblsp vegetable stock

Cut a slice from the top of ea pepper; scoop out the centre Heat the oil and fry the onion 2 minutes. Add the garlic, tomatoes and green chili and fry for 2-3 minutes. Add the potato, salt and pepper, peas lemon juice and parsley. Cove cook for 2-4 minutes. Arrang peppers in an ovenproof dish stuff the peppers with the rice mixture. Pour the stock aroun peppers. Bake at 375°F for 2C minutes, basting occasionally the juices. Serve hot.

Stuffed Tomatoes

Tomatoes stuffed with a vege filling and served with a tangy sauce make a good starter.

PREPARATION TIME: 20 mi

COOKING TIME: 15-18 minut

SERVES: 6 people

12 medium size firm tomatoes
2½ tblsp oil
10-12 scallions (only the white chopped
2½ tsp chopped parsley or coria leaves
1 cup cooked rice
2½ tsp pine kernels, or skinned hazelnuts, chopped
2½ tsp roasted sesame seeds
¾ tsp salt
½ tsp freshly ground black pepp
½ tsp ground mixed spice
1 cup vegetable stock
2½ tsp comstarch
2½ tblsp lemon juice
1 egg, well beaten

**Stuffed Summer Squash (t
Vegetable Kebabs (center
right) and Stuffed Peppers
(bottom).**

Slice the tops off the tomatoes and scoop out the center pulp, leaving a ¾ inch "shell". Reserve the tomato pulp. Heat the oil in the frying pan and fry the onions for 2-3 minutes. Add the parsley, cooked rice, nuts, sesame seeds, salt and pepper and allspice. Add the tomato pulp and any juice which may have formed. Cook, uncovered, for 3-4 minutes, until most of the moisture has evaporated. Stuff the hollowed tomatoes with the rice mixture and arrange in a large frying pan. Add the stock and cook for 4 minutes. Remove the tomatoes. Bring the liquid back to the boil and add the blended cornstarch and lemon juice. Remove from the heat. Add the beaten egg a little at a time. Return the mixture to the heat and cook until thickened. Add the stuffed tomatoes and cook over a low heat for 5 minutes, spooning the sauce over the tomatoes from time to time.

Fritters
(TEMPURA)

This is a Japanese dish and is very popular. The batter may be used for meats as well.

PREPARATION TIME: 10 minutes

COOKING TIME: 10-15 minutes

SERVES: 4 people

Batter
225g (8oz) all purpose flour
15ml (1 tblsp) cornstarch
¼ tsp salt
1 cup chilled water
1 egg yolk
2 egg whites, stiffly beaten

Oil for deep frying
1 cup fresh green beans, cut into 2 inch pieces
10-12 fresh asparagus spears, cut in 2 inch lengths
1 eggplant, cut into 1 inch cubes
1 large potato, peeled and sliced ¼ inch thick
10-12 fresh mushrooms, halved
6-8 cauliflower flowerets, halved

Tempura sauce: A
1 cup water
¼ cup sherry
¼ cup soya sauce
1¼ tsp sugar
½ a vegetable stock cube

Mix the ingredients together and bring to the boil. Stir until dissolved.

Tempura sauce: B
1 inch fresh root ginger, peeled and grated
2½ tblsp grated turnip

2½ tblsp grated radish
¼ cup prepared mustard
¼ cup soya sauce

Mix the ingredients together and keep covered.

To make the batter: mix together the flour, cornstarch and salt. Make a well in the center. Mix the chilled water and egg yolk together and pour into the center of the flour. Stir in the flour and blend lightly. Fold in the whisked egg whites.

Heat oil for deep frying. Dip the vegetables into the batter and fry in hot oil for 2-3 minutes until golden. Drain on kitchen paper and serve hot with the Tempura sauces. Use the batter within a few minutes of making. Do not allow it to stand for long.

Cheese and Lentil Balls

PREPARATION TIME: 30 minutes

COOKING TIME: 1 hour

SERVES: 4 people

1½ cups red lentils
1½ cups water
1 cup grated cheese
1 medium onion, peeled and chopped
2 large eggs
½ cup fresh breadcrumbs
1½ tsp mixed dried herbs
1½ tblsp lemon juice
Salt to taste
½ tsp freshly ground black pepper
Oil for shallow frying

Wash the lentils in 3-4 changes of water. Drain the lentils and put them into a pan with the water. Cook until the lentils are tender and the water has been absorbed. Remove from heat and allow to cool. Mix the cooked lentils with the cheese, onion, egg, breadcrumbs, herbs, salt and pepper and the lemon juice. Mix well and shape into balls. Shallow fry the balls for 4-5 minutes on each side until golden brown. Drain on absorbent paper and serve immediately.

Mixed Nut Rissoles

PREPARATION TIME: 15 minutes

COOKING TIME: 20-25 minutes

SERVES: 4 people

2 tblsp hazelnuts, chopped
½ cup shelled peanuts, chopped
½ cup cashew nuts, chopped

2 tblsp pistachio nuts, chopped
1 onion, peeled and chopped
¾ cup fresh breadcrumbs
3 eggs, beaten
Salt and freshly ground black pepper to taste
¾ tsp dried, chopped marjoram
1 carrot, peeled and grated
1¼ tblsp lemon juice
Little milk
Oil for shallow frying

Mix the chopped nuts with the onion, breadcrumbs, eggs, salt and pepper, marjoram, carrot and lemon juice. Add a little milk to bind the mixture, if necessary. Shape into rissoles. Shallow fry the rissoles in oil, for 4-5 minutes on each side, until golden brown. Drain well on absorbent paper and serve immediately. Alternatively, brush the rissoles generously with oil, put them onto a cooky tray and bake in the oven at 425°F for 15 minutes. Turn the rissoles halfway through cooking and brush with extra oil.

Cashew Nut Pie

PREPARATION TIME: 20-25 minutes

COOKING TIME: 30-40 minutes

SERVES: 4 people

Filling
2 medium onions, peeled and chopped
2 tblsp oil
2 cups shredded cabbage
½ cup carrots, peeled and grated

Pie Crust
1 cup crushed cornflakes
½ cup cashew nuts, coarsely ground
1½ cup grated cheese
1 tsp mixed dried herbs
Salt and freshly ground black pepper to taste
2 large eggs
1 cup fresh breadcrumbs
1 tblsp oil
¼ cup butter

To make the filling: fry the onions in the oil for 2 minutes; add the cabbage and carrots and fry for a further 4-5 minutes. Remove from the heat and allow to cool.

To make the pie crust: mix all the ingredients together in a bowl, apart from the oil, butter and ½ cup of the grated cheese. Grease a cake pan with the oil. Press half the pie crust ingredients out to form an even base. Spread the filling mixture on top, and then press over the remaining pie crust ingredients. Sprinkle with the

remaining grated cheese and do with butter. Bake in oven at 40 for 25-30 minutes.

Tomato, Onion and Mushroom Flan

PREPARATION TIME: 20 minu

COOKING TIME: 40-45 minut

SERVES: 6 people

8oz basic pastry
2 cups grated Cheddar cheese
4 tomatoes, skinned and choppe
1¼ tblsp chopped chives or parsle
1 cup mushrooms, sliced
2½ tsp corn oil
1 large onion, peeled and chopped
3 eggs, beaten
1⅔ cup milk
¾ tsp salt
½ tsp freshly ground black pepper

Roll out the pastry and use to li 8-9 inch flan dish. Put ¼ cup of grated cheese into the pastry ca followed by the tomatoes, chive parsley and the mushrooms. H the corn oil and fry the onion fo 3 minutes. Mix the beaten eggs with the milk, salt and pepper a fried onion. Pour into the flan ca and top with the remaining grat cheese. Bake at 400°F for 35-40 minutes, or until set. Serve hot cold.

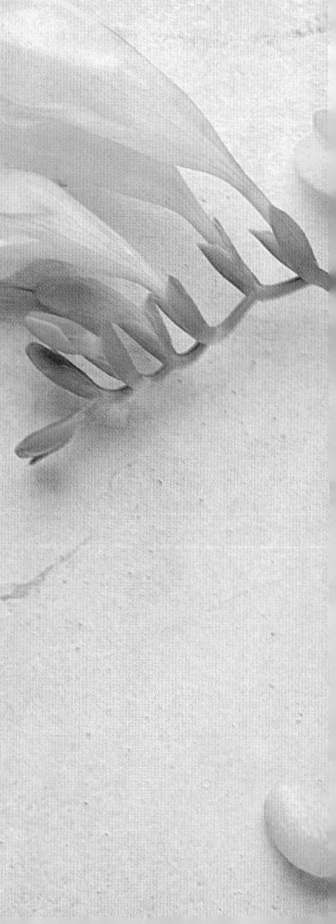

Mixed Nut Rissoles (left), Cheese and Lentil Rissoles (below) and Cashew Nut Pie (bottom).

Pakora

This is the Indian version of vegetable fritters. Fried with or without batter, they make an interesting starter or snack.

PREPARATION TIME: 15 minutes

COOKING TIME: 15-20 minutes

SERVES: 4-6 people

1 large potato, or
2 medium potatoes, peeled and cut into ¼ inch thick slices
8-10 cauliflower flowerets, halved lengthways
6 carrots, cut into 2 inch lengths and halved
1 eggplant, cut into 2 inch cubes
6 zucchini, trimmed and cut into 2 inch pieces and then quartered
1-2 green peppers, seeded and cut into ¼ inch) thick rounds or 1 inch pieces
1¼ tsp salt
1¼ tsp red chili powder
¾ tsp turmeric powder
Oil for deep frying
6 lemon wedges

Sprinkle the vegetables with the spices and rub well in. Keep on one side. Heat the oil for deep frying. When it is beginning to smoke, reduce the heat. Fry the vegetables a few at a time, in batches. Fry for 2-3 minutes and drain on kitchen paper. Serve piping hot with wedges of lemon and a sweet and sour chutney or tomato ketchup. (These uncoated fritters are called Bhaja).

Batter

2½ cups bessan flour, sieved (made from chick-peas)
1¼ tsp salt
1¼ tsp chili powder
1¼ tsp ground cumin
1 tblsp lemon juice
1¼ cups water

Mix the sieved flour with the salt, chili powder, cumin and lemon juice. Make a well in the centre and add the water; stir in the bessan flour until all the flour has been incorporated. Beat well to give a smooth batter. Adjust seasoning. Allow the batter to stand for a few minutes. Heat the oil as above. Dip the vegetables into the batter and then fry for 2-3 minutes. Drain on kitchen paper and serve piping hot with tomato sauce. Other vegetables which may be used: onions rings, raw banana slices, green tomato slices, spinach leaves.

Stuffed Mushrooms

PREPARATION TIME: 20 minutes

COOKING TIME: 10-15 minutes

SERVES: 4-6 people

Filling

1 small onion, peeled and finely chopped
2½ tsp oil
½ inch fresh root ginger, peeled and crushed
2 cloves garlic, peeled and crushed
2 cups boiled, peeled and mashed potatoes
Salt and freshly ground black pepper to taste
1¼ tblsp lemon juice
2½ tsp chopped chives or parsley

20-24 large mushrooms
1½ cup grated Cheddar cheese
Oil for brushing

Fry the onion in the 2½ tsp oil for 2 minutes; add the ginger and garlic. Fry for 1 minute and mix with the mashed potatoes. Season to taste with salt, pepper, lemon juice and chopped parsley. Mix well. Remove the stalks from the mushrooms; stuff the hollows with the potato filling and top with a little Cheddar cheese. Brush the mushrooms with a little oil and arrange them on a baking tray. Bake the mushrooms in a moderately hot oven, 375°F, for 10 minutes until the cheese is brown.

Aloo Bonda

This is an Indian potato fritter recipe made in the shape of spicy balls. Eaten hot or cold, they are ideal for parties, snacks and picnics.

PREPARATION TIME: 25 minu[tes]

COOKING TIME: 30 minutes

SERVES: 4-6 people

Batter

2 cups bessan flour, sieved (made from chick-peas)
½ tsp salt
½ tsp baking powder
1¼ cups water

1lb potatoes, boiled in their skins a[nd] peeled
1 large or 2 medium onions, peele[d] and chopped
1 inch fresh root ginger, peeled and finely chopped
2-3 green chilies, chopped
4-5 sprigs fresh green coriander leaves, chopped
¾ tsp salt
½ tsp freshly ground black pepper
1¼ tblsp lemon juice
Oil for deep frying

Mix the sieved flour with the sal[t] and baking powder. Make a well [in] the centre and add the water. Be[at] well to give a smooth batter. Ch[op] the boiled potatoes into tiny cu[be,] add the chopped onions, ginger, chilies, coriander leaves, salt and pepper to taste and lemon juice. Mix well and adjust seasoning to taste. Mold into even-sized balls with dampened hands. Heat the [oil] for deep frying. When hot, dip t[he] vegetable balls into the batter an[d] then fry for 3-4 minutes over a gentle heat until golden brown. Drain on kitchen paper and serv[e] with tomato sauce.

This page: Aloo Bonda (top)[,] Fritters (Tempura) (center right) and Pakora (bottom left).

Facing page: Stuffed Tomatoes (top right), Stuffed Mushrooms (center left) and Tomato, Onion and Mushroom Flan (bottom).

Salads

Onion Salad

This salad is usually served as an accompaniment to kebabs. Onion salad goes very well with a variety of main courses, as a side salad.

PREPARATION TIME: 5-7 minutes
SERVES: 4 people

2 large Spanish onions, peeled and
    thinly sliced
2-3 sprigs fresh green coriander,
    chopped
1 green chili, sliced
Juice of 1 lemon
¾ tsp salt
Pinch paprika

Combine the onion rings, coriander leaves and chili in a bowl. Add the lemon juice and salt and mix well. Put the onion salad onto a serving plate and sprinkle with paprika.

Tabbouleh

This is a Lebanese salad and it is very good for parties and picnics.

PREPARATION TIME: 2 hours
                                    30 minutes
SERVES: 6 people

2 cups bulgar or pourgouri
    (precooked, cracked wheat)
1 cup boiling water
8-10 scallions, chopped
1 green pepper, seeded and chopped
⅔ cup parsley
2½ tblsp chopped mint leaves

Dressing
¼ cup lemon juice
¾ cup olive oil
1¼ tsp grated lemon peel
1¼ tsp ground mixed spice
¾ tsp ground cumin
1¼ tsp salt
¼ tsp freshly ground black pepper
1 small iceberg lettuce, shredded
2 large firm tomatoes, cut into wedges
10-15 pitted black olives, halved
2-3 sprigs mint
1-2 sprigs fresh green coriander

Place the pourgouri or bulgar into a bowl and add boiling water. Cover and stand for 1½-2 hours. Drain the bulgar by squeezing out the excess water. Mix the scallions, green pepper, parsley and mint with the bulgar. Combine all the dressing ingredients in a screw top jar and shake well. Pour the dressing over the bulgar mixture and mix lightly. Line a platter with shredded lettuce. Place the prepared bulgar in the centre. Garnish with tomato, olives, mint and coriander leaves.

Sweet and Sour Coleslaw

A variation on the usual theme, but a definite winner.

PREPARATION TIME: 20 minutes
SERVES: 6 people

½ small red cabbage, shredded
1 small green cabbage, shredded
1 large sweet carrot, peeled and
    shredded
3 scallions, finely chopped
6½ tblsp cider vinegar
4 tblsp brown sugar
¾ tsp salt
½ tsp freshly ground black pepper
6½ tblsp soured cream
1¼ tsp French mustard

Combine the red and green cabbage, carrots and scallions in a mixing bowl. Mix the vinegar, sugar and salt and pepper in a small saucepan and stir over the heat to dissolve the sugar. Pour the hot vinegar sauce over the cabbage mixture and mix well. Stir the soured cream and mustard together in a separate bowl; stir this mixture into the vegetables. Mix well and serve.

Mixed Bean Salad

This nutritious salad is made from a medley of beans and is very good for health conscious and athletic people. Either cook the dried beans at home or buy ready-cooked ones. Soak the beans separately overnight, and then boil them separately until tender. Drain well.

PREPARATION TIME: 15 minutes
SERVES: 4-6 people

1½ cups cooked red kidney beans
1½ cups cooked black eyed beans
    (Lobia)
1½ cups cooked chick peas
1½ cups cooked butter beans
1 cup shelled broad beans
2 cups sliced green beans, blanched

Dressing
2½ tblsp brown sugar
½ cup white wine vinegar
¾ tsp salt
½ tsp freshly ground black pepper
½ cup olive oil
¾ tsp dry mustard powder
¾ tsp dried basil leaves
1 large Spanish or red onion, peeled
    and thinly sliced into rings
2½ tblsp parsley

Mix all the beans together in a large bowl. Mix the sugar and vinegar together with salt and pepper to taste. Stir in the oil, mustard and basil. Pour this vinegar mixture over the beans. Mix thoroughly. Refrigerate until ready to serve. Before serving, mix in the onion rings and parsley.

Nutty Salad

PREPARATION TIME: 20 minutes
SERVES: 4 people

4 cups boiled potatoes, diced
1½ cups shelled green peas
1 cup cooked carrots, diced
1 medium onion, peeled and chopped
1 small green pepper, seeded and
    chopped
8-10 radishes, chopped
2 stalks celery, chopped
¼ cucumber, chopped
½ cup roasted peanuts, coarsely
    chopped
½ cup grated fresh coconut
1¼ tblsp sunflower seeds
2-3 sprigs fresh green coriander leaves
    or parsley, chopped

Dressing
2½ tblsp lemon juice
5¼ tblsp olive oil
1¼ tsp salt

¾ tsp freshly ground black pepp[er]
1 tsp brown sugar

Mix all the vegetables togethe[r] except the nuts and sunflower seeds, in a large bowl. Mix the dressing ingredients together i[n a] screw top jar and shake well. A[dd] the dressing to the salad and m[ix] throughly. Sprinkle with the n[uts] and sunflower seeds before se[rving].

Rice and Nut Salad

This salad has a very refreshin[g] taste. The main ingredients ar[e] nuts, raisins, carrots and rice.

PREPARATION TIME: 15 min[utes]
SERVES: 4 people

2½ tblsp olive oil
2½ tblsp lemon juice
Salt and freshly ground black pe[pper]
    to taste
1 cup white raisins
½ cup currants
2½ cups cooked long grain rice,
    drained
¾ cup chopped blanched almo[nds]
½ cup cashew nuts, chopped
½ cup shelled walnuts, chopped
15oz can peach slices, drained a[nd]
    chopped
¼ cucumber, cubed
1 cup cooked red kidney beans
1¼ tblsp chopped pitted olives

Mix the olive oil, lemon juice a[nd] salt and freshly ground black pepper in a screw top jar; shak[e] vigorously. Soak the raisins an[d] currants in sufficient boiling w[ater] to cover, for 10 minutes. Drain [the] fruits. Mix the rice, nuts and soaked raisins and currants. A[dd] the chopped peaches, cucumb[er,] red kidney beans and olives. Po[ur] the dressing over the salad and [mix] lightly together. Serve on a be[d of] chopped lettuce.

**Facing page: Onion Salad
(top), Nutty Salad (center)
Tabbouleh (bottom).**

Cheese Salad

This cheese salad originates from Greece and has many variations; it is popularly known as Horiatiki.

PREPARATION TIME: 10-12 minutes

SERVES: 4 people

½ a head of chicory
½ iceberg lettuce
1 cucumber, peeled and sliced
3-4 large tomatoes, cut into wedges, or
15-20 baby tomatoes, halved
8-10 pitted green or black olives, halved
1 medium Spanish or red onion, peeled and chopped
1 cup Feta cheese, cut into ½ inch pieces

Dressing
⅓ cup olive oil
2½ tblsp red wine vinegar
1½ tsp chopped fresh oregano or
½ tsp dried oregano
¾ tsp salt
½ tsp freshly ground black pepper
¾ tsp brown sugar

Wash and dry the chicory and lettuce leaves; tear into bite size pieces. Place the chicory and lettuce in a large bowl and add the cucumber, tomatoes, olives, onion and cheese. Shake the dressing ingredients together in a screw top jar. Pour the dressing over the salad. Toss lightly and serve.

Cheese Salad (bottom left), Mixed Bean Salad (below) and Rice and Nut Salad (bottom right).

Mixed Fresh Vegetable Salad

This salad can be prepared with any combination of vegetables, in any proportion. Add or subtract according to personal taste.

PREPARATION TIME: 20 minutes

SERVES: 6 people

1 large scallion, peeled and chopped
½ cucumber, diced
3 carrots, peeled and diced
6 large tomatoes, diced, or
8 baby tomatoes, halved
10 mushrooms, diced
3 stalks celery, diced
1 green pepper, seeded and diced
15-20 tiny cauliflower flowerets
15-20 radishes, quartered
1¼ tblsp chopped watercress or
    mustard and cress
2 sprigs fresh green coriander leaves
    or parsley, chopped

Dressing
½ tsp salt
½ tsp freshly ground black pepper
1¼ tsp brown sugar
2½ tsp cider vinegar
1¼ tblsp lemon juice
1¼ tblsp honey
5¼ tblsp olive oil
Pinch mustard powder
8 lettuce leaves

Combine all the vegetables in a large bowl. Mix together all the dressing ingredients. Pour the dressing over the vegetables and serve on a bed of lettuce leaves.

Pasta Salad

This is a popular American salad. It can be eaten as a main dish or as a side salad – it is a wonderful combination of vegetables, pasta and kidney beans.

PREPARATION TIME: 15-20 minutes

SERVES: 6 people

4 cups cooked red kidney beans, drained
3 cups pasta shells or spirals, cooked
1 large green pepper, seeded and sliced into 1 inch long pieces
1 large red pepper, seeded and sliced into 1 inch long pieces
20-30 pitted black olives, sliced in half
1 tblsp capers
4-5 sprigs fresh parsley, chopped

Dressing
1 cup olive oil
¼ cup lemon juice
2½ tsp finely chopped fresh basil leaves
1¼ tsp salt
½ tsp freshly ground black pepper
2 cloves garlic, peeled and minced
1 small head chicory

Combine the beans, pasta, peppers, olives, capers and parsley in a large bowl. Mix all the dressing ingredients together; add to the salad ingredients and toss together. Line the serving platter or bowl with chicory leaves; place the pasta salad in the centre. Alternatively: add ½lb of thinly sliced salami or Italian sausages or can sausages in brine cut into bite size pieces.

This page: Sweet and Sour Coleslaw (top left), Mixed Fresh Vegetable Salad (top right) and Pasta Salad (bottom).

Facing page: Kedgeree (top left), Sweet Savory Rice (center right) and Vegetable Pulao Rice (bottom).

Rice and Pulses

...dgeree

...PARATION TIME: 15 minutes,
...soaking time
...KING TIME: 30 minutes
...ES: 4-6 people

...s long grain rice
...s red lentils
...s tepid water
...ck of butter (or an equivalent
...mount of olive oil)
...dium onion, peeled and chopped
...o crushed fresh root ginger
...o crushed garlic
...h piece cinnamon stick
...ves
...leaf
...p ground coriander
...o ground turmeric
...o salt
...en chilies, sliced in half
...ngthwise

...h the rice and the lentils in 4 to
...anges of water; soak them in
...3 cups tepid water for 30
...utes. Heat the butter or oil in a
...e pan; add the onion and fry for
...minutes. Add the ginger, garlic,
...amon stick, cloves and bayleaf,
...fry for 1 minute. Drain the
...er from the rice and lentils;
...rve the water. Add the rice and
...ls to the fried onion, together
...the coriander, turmeric, salt
...green chilies. Stir over the heat
...-3 minutes, until the rice and
...ls are evenly coated with fat.
...the reserved water and bring
...e boil; reduce the heat and
...ner covered for 8-10 minutes,
...out stirring, until the water has
...absorbed and the rice and
...ls are tender. Serve with a
...table curry.

...getable Pulao Rice

...PARATION TIME: 30 minutes
...KING TIME: 30 minutes
...VES: 4-6 people

...ps long grain rice (Basmati)
...cups water
...dium onion, peeled and diced
...h piece cinnamon stick
...yleaf

6 cloves
1¼ tsp black cumin (shah-zeera)
6 small cardamoms
¾ tsp crushed fresh root ginger
¾ tsp crushed garlic
1 medium potato, peeled and diced
1 carrot, peeled and diced
1 cup shelled peas
¾ cup sliced green beans
1¼ tsp garam masala powder (hot aromatic powder)
¾ tsp chili powder
1¼ tsp ground coriander
1¼ tsp ground cumin
1¼ tsp salt
2½ tblsp lemon juice
A stick of butter (or an equivalent amount of olive oil)

Wash the rice in 4-5 changes of water and soak in the 3-4 cups water for 30 minutes. Melt the butter in a pan and fry the onion for 2-3 minutes. Add the cinnamon, bayleaf, cloves, black cumin, cardamoms, ginger and garlic. Fry for 1 minute, stirring, and add the potato, carrot, peas, green beans, garam masala, chili, coriander, cumin and salt. Mix well. Drain the soaked rice, retaining the water and add the rice to the onion and spices. Stir the mixture gently and add the reserved water. Bring to the boil and then reduce the heat; cover and simmer gently for 10-15 minutes, until the rice is tender and the water has been absorbed. Do not stir during cooking. Sprinkle with the lemon juice and serve. To colour pulao: dissolve a pinch of saffron in 1¼ tblsp warm milk; pour over the rice and allow to stand over a very low heat for 5 minutes.

Mixed Daal

This is a mixed lentil stew, using 3 or 4 varieties of daal. Add a few vegetables of your choice to turn it into a substantial meal.

PREPARATION TIME: 15 minutes
COOKING TIME: 30 minutes
SERVES: 4 people

⅔ cup split Bengal grain (Channa)
½ cup yellow lentils (Toor Daal)
1 cup red lentils (Masoor)
½ cup dehusked split mung (Moong), or any other daal
¾ tsp ground turmeric
1¾ tsp ground coriander
4 canned tomatoes, chopped
2 green chilies
3 sprigs fresh green coriander leaves

Salt to taste
A stick of butter
½ inch fresh root ginger, peeled and chopped
1 onion, chopped
1 clove garlic, chopped

As some of these pulses have different cooking times, wash each pulse separately in 3-4 changes of water. Drain. Soak separately in water for 5 minutes. Bring 2½ cups water to the boil; add the drained channa daal. Boil for 15-20 minutes or until the pulses are tender. Add the remaining pulses well drained, and simmer gently with the turmeric and ground coriander for 15-20 minutes, or until all the pulses are soft. Beat with an egg whisk. Add the tomatoes, green chilies and coriander leaves. Simmer for a further 5-6 minutes. Pour into a serving bowl and keep warm. Melt the butter in a frying pan and fry the ginger for 2 minutes. Add the onion and garlic and fry until golden brown. Pour this mixture over the mixed daal and serve immediately.

Sweet Savory Rice

PREPARATION TIME: 20 minutes
COOKING TIME: 30 minutes
SERVES: 4-6 people

4 cups rice (Basmati or long grain)
3-4 cups water
½ cup raisins
¾ cup cashew nuts, chopped
½ cup blanched almonds, split
½ cup pistachio nuts, split
A stick of butter (or an equivalent amount of olive oil)
1 inch piece cinnamon stick
6 cloves
6 small cardamoms
1 bayleaf
¾ tsp black cumin seed (shah-zeera)
1 cup white raisins
1¼ tsp salt
1¼ tsp sugar
Pinch of saffron

Wash the rice in 4-5 changes of water and soak in the 3-4 cups water for 30 minutes. Soak the raisins and nuts in a little water for 10 minutes. Drain the raisins and nuts. Melt the butter in a large pan and fry the cinnamon, cloves, small cardamoms, bayleaf and black cumin for 1-2 minutes. Add the nuts and all raisins. Drain the soaked rice retaining the water; add

the rice to the saucepan. Fry for 1 minute. Add salt, sugar and the reserved water. Bring to the boil. Reduce the heat and add a pinch of saffron. Stir once gently. Cover and simmer gently for 10-15 minutes, without stirring, until the rice is tender and the water has been absorbed. Serve with curries.

Red Kidney Bean Curry

A popular dish from the Punjab province of India. It is similar to Chilli Con-Carne and makes a hearty meal with bread or rice.

PREPARATION TIME: overnight, plus 15 minutes
COOKING TIME: 20-45 minutes
SERVES: 4 people

2 cups dried red kidney beans, washed and soaked overnight in sufficient water to cover
2 medium onions, chopped
4 tblsp oil
1 bayleaf
1 inch piece cinnamon stick
6 cloves
6 small green cardamoms
2 green chilies, quartered
3 cloves garlic, peeled and finely chopped
1 inch fresh root ginger, peeled and finely chopped
¾ tsp chili powder
¼ tsp ground turmeric
2 tsp ground coriander
1¼ tsp ground cumin
1¼ tsp garam masala powder (hot aromatic powder)
15oz can peeled tomatoes, chopped
¾ tsp salt
2-3 sprigs fresh green coriander, chopped

Either pressure cook the red kidney beans for 5-6 minutes, or cook them in their soaking water for 15-20 minutes until soft. Remove from the heat; allow to stand, covered. Fry the onions in the oil in a large saucepan over a moderate heat until tender. Add the bayleaf, cinnamon, cloves and cardamoms and fry for 1 minute. Add the chilies, garlic and ginger and fry until golden. Sprinkle with the chili powder, turmeric, ground coriander, ground cumin and garam masala. Avoid burning the mixture. Stir the mixture to blend the spices. Add the tomatoes and season with salt. Cover and

simmer for 2-3 minutes. Drain cooked beans and collect the red liquid. Add the beans to the spiced tomato mixture. Stir ge and cook for 1 minute. Add th liquid and chopped coriander; cover and simmer for 3-5 min Serve with bread or boiled rice

Red Lentil Daal

There is an abundance of natu protein in pulses and there is a great variety of pulses now available.

PREPARATION TIME: 10 min
COOKING TIME: 30 minutes
SERVES: 4 people

½lb red lentils
1½ cups water
½ tsp ground turmeric
1¼ tsp ground coriander
1 green chili, cut in half
Salt to taste
4-6 canned tomatoes, chopped
2 sprigs fresh green coriander lea chopped
4 tblsp butter
1 small onion, peeled and finely chopped

Wash the lentils in 3-5 change water. Put the lentils into a par with the 1½ cups water; cover cook over a low heat for 10-15 minutes. Remove any froth wi spoon. Once the lentils are ten and yellow, blend until smooth with an egg whisk. Add the turmeric, ground coriander, ch salt to taste and chopped toma Cover and simmer for 10 minu Add the coriander leaves and p into a dish. Keep warm. Melt t butter in a frying pan and saute onion until golden brown. Pou onions and butter juices over t daal. Serve with rice or bread.

Facing page: Mixed Daal (t left), Red Kidney Bean Cur (center) and Red Lentil Daa (bottom).

Bread and Pizza

Puri

These deep-fried breads are simple to make once the art has been mastered.

PREPARATION TIME:	10-15 minutes
COOKING TIME:	20 minutes
MAKES:	30-32

4 cups whole-wheat flour
¾ tsp salt
1-1½ cups water
Oil for deep frying

Sieve the flour and salt into a mixing bowl. Mix to a soft dough with water. Knead well and leave to relax for 5 minutes, covered with a damp cloth. Divide the dough in 30-32 small even sized balls; roll out each ball into a small round about 2½-3 inches in diameter. Heat the oil for deep frying and drop in a small piece of dough. I rises to the top instantly then th correct temperature for frying ha been reached. Place one puri at time into the hot oil, taking care not to splash the oil. Gently stir puri and it will begin to swell. T over and cook on the underside until golden brown – about ½-1 minute. The flip side is always th thick side and it needs extra cooking time. Drain the puris o the side of the frying pan, and p them on kitchen paper to drain.

Puri (above), Roti (right) and Paratha (far right).

fore serving. Puris are best when
ved piping hot. Puris can be
ved cold and they can also be
eated under the broiler.

ratha

ese shallow-fried breads can
her be made plain, or stuffed
th a favorite filling, such as
eese, potato etc.

EPARATION TIME: 15-20
minutes

OOKING TIME: 20-30 minutes

AKES: 16-18

4 cups whole-wheat flour
¾ tsp salt
1-1½ cups water
Melted butter or oil

Sieve the flour and salt into a
mixing bowl. Mix to a soft dough
with water. Knead the dough well;
leave to relax, covered, for 5
minutes. Divide the dough into 16-
18 even-sized balls. Roll each ball
into a small round about 2 inches
in diameter. Brush each round of
dough with oil or melted butter
and fold in half. Brush the upper
folded surface with oil or butter
and fold in half to form a small
triangle. On a well floured surface
roll out these triangles thinly. Heat
a solid based frying pan or a
griddle. Put the paratha onto the
heated frying pan and cook for ½-1
minute or until small brown specks
appear. Cook the other side in the
same way. Brush a little oil or
butter over the paratha and turn
over. Fry for 1 minute and then
brush the second side with oil or
butter. Fry on both sides until the

paratha is golden and crisp. Make the rest of the paratha in the same way. Keep them soft and warm, well wrapped in a clean tea towel or foil.

Roti

Roti is best made with whole-wheat flour; any variety may be used.

PREPARATION TIME: 20 minutes	
COOKING TIME: 20-30 minutes	
MAKES: about 24	

4 cups whole-wheat flour
¾ tsp salt
1-1½ cups water

Sieve the flour and salt into a mixing bowl. Mix to a soft dough with water. Knead the dough for 2-3 minutes. Cover and allow to relax for 5-6 minutes before shaping the bread. Divide the dough into 1oz balls. Roll each ball into a thin round about 5-6 inches in diameter. Place a solid based frying pan or a griddle over a medium heat; when the pan is hot, place the shaped roti onto it. Cook for ½ minute on each side and then place under a preheated broiler to bloat (little brown specks will appear on the surface). The first 2 rotis do not usually bloat, so do not be alarmed. Make all the rotis and stack them one on top of each other. Keep them covered with a clean tea towel or foil. Serve hot with any curry or spicy savory dish.

Banana and Nut Bread

PREPARATION TIME: 30 minutes	
COOKING TIME: 1 hour	
MAKES: 1 loaf	

A stick of butter
1 cup brown sugar
1 egg, well beaten
2 cups whole-wheat flour
½ tsp salt
¾ tsp baking powder
5 tblsp natural yogurt
2 ripe bananas, peeled and mashed
½ cup raisins
1 cup mixed nuts, chopped

Preheat the oven to 350°F. Cream the butter and sugar until light and fluffy and gradually beat in the egg. Sieve the flour, salt and baking powder together. Add half the yogurt to the butter and sugar mixture and then mix in half the sieved dry ingredients. Beat in the remaining yogurt, flour, mashed banana, raisins and chopped nuts. Mix well. Put the mixture into a greased loaf tin. Bake at 350°F for 1 hour.

Crusty Loaf

PREPARATION TIME: 3 hours 40 minutes	
COOKING TIME: 45 minutes- 1 hour	
MAKES: 2 loaves	

1¼ cups tepid water
½oz fresh yeast or 2½ tsp dried yeast
¾ tsp salt
1 tblsp butter
1¼ tblsp sugar
3½ cups sieved all purpose flour
1¼ tblsp melted butter
1½ tblsp caraway, sesame or poppy seeds for topping (optional)

Sprinkle or crumble the yeast into the tepid water; stir to dissolve. Leave for a few minutes until frothy. Mix the salt, butter, sugar and flour together; stir in the yeast liquid and mix to a dough. Knead the dough for 10 minutes on a lightly floured surface. Place the dough in a greased bowl and brush the top lightly with melted butter; cover with a damp cloth and leave it to rise in a warm place (free from draught), until doubled in bulk (about 40-45 minutes). Punch the dough down and let it rise again until almost double its original size about (30 minutes). Punch down once again and turn out onto a floured surface, cut into two equal portions. Roll each one into an oblong about 8-10 inches in length. Beginning with the wide side, roll up each oblong tightly. Seal the edges by pinching together. Holding each end of the roll, roll it gently backwards and forwards to lengthen the loaf and shape the ends. Place the loaves on a greased baking sheet lightly sprinkled with all purpose flour. Brush the loaves either with milk, or with cornstarch glaze, and leave to rise for 1½ hours, uncovered. With a sharp knife, make ¼ inch slashes at regular intervals. Bake in a hot oven, 400°F, for 10 minutes. Brush once again with milk or cornstarch glaze and sprinkle with poppy seeds (or other seeds). Return to the oven and bake for 25-30 minutes

or until golden brown.

To make cornstarch glaze: mix 1½ tsp cornstarch with 1½ tsp cold water. Add ½ cup boiling water and cook for 1-2 minutes until smooth. Cool slightly before use.

Whole-wheat Bread

PREPARATION TIME: 2 hours 30 minutes	
COOKING TIME: 50 minutes	
MAKES: 1 large loaf	

6 cups whole-wheat flour
¾ tsp salt
¼ cup margarine
¼ cup fresh yeast, or
1¼ tblsp dried yeast (see below)
1¼ tblsp granulated or brown sugar
1¼ cups tepid water
⅔ cup tepid milk
1¼ tblsp melted butter

Sieve the flour and salt into a warm bowl and blend the margarine. Cream the fresh yeast with the sugar and stir in the warm water and milk. (If using dried yeast, sprinkle it onto the warm water and milk, with the sugar, and leave to stand for 10 minutes until thick and frothy). Make a well in the centre of the flour and pour in the yeast liquid; gradually mix in the flour to form a dough. Knead the dough well. Cover it with a damp cloth and leave to rise until double in bulk (about 1¼ hours). Grease a loaf tin, 9 inches by 5 inches by 3 inches. Turn the risen dough onto a floured surface and knead well; place in the loaf tin. Leave in a warm place to rise for 40 minutes. Brush the loaf with melted butter and bake at 400°F for about 50 minutes.

Whole-wheat Pizza Dough

PREPARATION TIME: 50-60 minutes	

1 cup tepid water
1¾ tsp dried yeast
¾ tsp salt
1¼ tsp sugar

1¼ tsp olive oil
1 cup whole-wheat flour
1¼ cups all purpose flour

Mix the dried yeast with the water. Add the salt, sugar and Mix in the flours a little at a t to make a dough. Use extra w needed. Turn the dough onto lightly floured surface and kne until smooth (about 5-8 min Cover the dough with a clean damp tea towel and leave to s for 15-20 minutes. Knead onc more for 1-2 minutes. You car make either one large pizza ba several smaller ones. Grease c inch pizza pan and roll out th dough to make a round large enough to fit the pizza pan. Sl the pizza dough with the hand fit the pan. Top with the chos topping and bake.

Basic Pizza Dough

This is the basic recipe for piz dough and although there are many variations, the making c dough is very important. Pizz originated in Italy, around the Naples area, but it is now eate enjoyed worldwide. Once the dough is perfected, toppings c adjusted to one's taste. In fact one single pizza, each slice car a different taste (i.e. with a di topping). See Taco Pizza Topp and Mixed Vegetable Pizza To recipes.

PREPARATION TIME: about 1 hour 30 minutes	

¼ tsp sugar
1¼ tblsp dried yeast
½ cup tepid water
1¼ tsp salt
2 cups all purpose flour, sieved

Mix the dried yeast with 2 tb the tepid water and the sugar. until dissolved. Leave to stand 10-15 minutes until frothy. Pu flour and salt into a bowl and

Facing page: Crusty Loaf (top), Banana and Nut Bre (center) and Whole-whea Bread (bottom).

a well in the centre. Add the yeast liquid and the remaining tepid water; mix to form a dough. Knead the dough on a floured surface for 8-10 minutes. Cover with a damp cloth and leave to rise in a warm place for 40-45 minutes, until double its original size. Knead once again on a lightly floured surface for 3-5 minutes until soft and elastic. You can make either one large pizza base, or several smaller ones. Grease one 14 inch pizza pan and roll out the dough. Shape the pizza dough with the hands to fit the pan. Top with the chosen topping and bake.

Taco Pizza

This idea is taken from the taco (a Mexican pancake). The pizza base is made with a mixture of cornmeal and flour and some of the topping ingredients are the same as those used in a taco filling.

PREPARATION TIME: 30-40 minutes	
COOKING TIME: 30-35 minutes	
SERVES: 6 people	

Dough
1½ cups all purpose flour
⅔ cup fine yellow cornmeal
2½ tsp baking powder
1¼ tsp salt
½ cup margarine
½ cup milk

Sieve the flour, cornmeal, salt and baking powder into a mixing bowl. Rub in the margarine. Add the milk, gradually, to form a medium soft dough. Knead the dough on a well floured surface for 4-5 minutes, until smooth. Roll into a circle to cover a 13-14 inch pizza pan, with a 1 inch high rim. Grease the pizza pan and cover with the dough. Shape the pizza dough to fit the pan. Pinch the edges to form a deep rim. Keep on one side until the topping is ready.

Topping
2½ tblsp olive oil
1 clove garlic, peeled and crushed
1 small onion, peeled and chopped
½ green pepper, seeded and coarsely chopped
4-6 mushrooms, sliced
½lb cooked red kidney beans (or drained canned ones)
2 scallions, chopped
3 large tomatoes, chopped
6-8 pitted black olives, halved
3-4 pickled Mexican chilies, chopped
½lb Mozzarella, Cheddar or Monterey Jack cheese, cut into slivers
1 carrot, peeled and grated
⅔ cup soured cream
Bottled taco sauce

Heat the oil and fry the garlic, chopped onion, pepper and mushrooms for 2 minutes; add the kidney beans and stir fry for 1-2 minutes. Remove from the heat and stir in the scallions. Spread the above topping mixture over the pizza base. Arrange the tomatoes evenly on top. Add the olives, Mexican chilies and slivers of cheese. Bake at 400°F for 15-20 minutes until the edges turn golden brown and crusty. Serve with grated carrots, whipped soured cream and taco sauce.

Mixed Vegetable Pizza Topping

PREPARATION TIME: 30 minutes	
COOKING TIME: 20 minutes	
SERVES: 4-6 people	

2½ tblsp olive oil
1 small onion, peeled and chopped
2 scallions, chopped
1 medium zucchini, trimmed and thinly sliced
4 mushrooms, sliced
Salt and freshly ground black pepper to taste
6-8 canned tomatoes, chopped
10ml (2 tsp) tomato paste
8 pitted black olives
2 tomatoes, thinly sliced
1 green pepper, seeded and chopped
1 green chili, chopped
1¼ tsp dried oregano
1½ cups Mozzarella cheese, Cheddar cheese or a mixture of the two, cut into thin slivers
2½ tblsp grated Parmesan cheese

Heat the olive oil in a large frying pan; add the onions and sauté for 1-2 minutes. Add the zucchini and sauté for 2 minutes. Add the mushrooms and salt and pepper to taste and stir fry for 1 minute to glaze the vegetables. Remove from the heat and cool. Mix the chopped tomato with the tomato paste and spread evenly over the pizza base. Spoon the vegetable mixture over the pizza and arrange the olives, sliced tomatoes, green pepper and green chili on top. Sprinkle with the oregano, the slivers of cheese and the grated Parmesan cheese. Bake at 450°F for 12-15 minutes, or until the edge of the pizza is golden brown and crusty.

Taco Pizza (top right) and Mixed Vegetable Pizza Topping (bottom right).

Main Meals

Okra Curry

A dry vegetable curry made with okra and potato.

PREPARATION TIME: 10-15 minutes

COOKING TIME: 30 minutes

SERVES: 4 people

3¾ tblsp oil
1 onion, peeled and chopped
2 medium sized potatoes, peeled and
    cut into 1 inch pieces
4 cups okra, topped and tailed, and
    chopped into ½inch pieces
Salt to taste
¾ tsp ground turmeric
1¼ tsp chili powder
1¾ tsp ground coriander
2-3 sprigs fresh green coriander
    leaves, chopped

Heat the oil in a wok or solid based frying pan and fry the onion for 3-4 minutes. Stir in the cubed potatoes; cover and cook for 3-4 minutes. Add the okra, and stir fry for 2 minutes. Sprinkle with salt to taste, turmeric, chili and ground coriander. Mix gently; cover and cook for 8-10 minutes. Stir occasionally and continue cooking until the potatoes are tender. Sprinkle with the chopped coriander leaves. Mix well and serve.

Okra Fry

This is a dry "curry" – no spices are added; the okra supplies the hotness.

PREPARATION TIME: 15 minutes

COOKING TIME: 20-30 minutes

SERVES: 4 people

1-1½lbs okra
Oil for deep frying
1¼ tblsp oil
1 large onion, peeled and chopped
Salt and freshly ground black pepper
    to taste

Top and tail the okra; chop them into ¼ inch even-sized pieces. Heat the oil for deep frying; add the chopped okra, a little at a time, and deep fry until brown and crisp. Drain on absorbent paper and keep warm in a dish. Heat the 1¼ tblsp oil and fry the onion until tender about 4-5 minutes. Remove the onion and mix with the fried okra. Sprinkle with salt and pepper to taste. Serve with chapati, or as a side dish.

Eggplant Bake

PREPARATION TIME: 30 minutes

COOKING TIME: 30-40 minutes

SERVES: 6 people

3 large eggplant
2½ tsp salt
Malt vinegar
2½ tblsp oil
2 large onions, peeled and sliced
2 green chilies, chopped
15oz can peeled tomatoes, chopped
¾ tsp chili powder
1¼ tsp crushed garlic
¾ tsp ground turmeric
Oil for deep frying
⅓ cup natural yogurt
1¼ tsp freshly ground black pepper
4 tomatoes, sliced
2 cups Cheddar cheese, grated

Cut the eggplant into ¼ inch thick slices. Lay in a shallow dish. Sprinkle with 1¼ tsp salt and add sufficient malt vinegar to cover. Allow to marinate for 20-30 minutes. Drain well. Heat 2½ tblsp oil in a frying pan and fry the onions until golden brown. Add the chilies, chopped tomatoes, remaining salt, chili powder, garlic and turmeric. Mix well and simmer for 5-7 minutes. Remove from the heat. Cool and blend to a smooth sauce in the liquidizer. Keep the sauce on one side. Heat the oil for deep frying and deep fry the drained, marinated eggplant until brown on both sides (2-3 minutes each side). Drain well on kitchen paper. Grease a large deep baking tray. Arrange half the fried eggplant rounds closely together in the tray. Spoon over half the tomato sauce and beaten yogurt. Season with pepper. Add the remaining eggplant rounds and the rest of the tomato sauce and yogurt. Cover with slices of tomatoes and grated cheese. Bake at 350°F for 10-15 minutes, or until the cheese melts and turns brown. Serve hot as a side dish, or as a main course with brown bread or pitta bread.

Stuffed Zucchini

This is a delightful dish from Southern Italy.

PREPARATION TIME: 30 minutes

COOKING TIME: 30-40 minutes

SERVES: 4 people

½ cup fresh coarse breadcrumbs
5 tblsp milk
8 medium sized zucchini, trimmed
1 onion, peeled and finely chopped
2 tomatoes, chopped
6-8 mushrooms, sliced
1 clove garlic, peeled and chopped
5 tblsp olive oil
2½ tsp dried oregano
Salt and freshly ground black pepper
    to taste
1 egg, beaten
⅔ cup Mozzarella cheese (or
    Cheddar), cut into thin slivers
⅔ cup grated Parmesan cheese

Soak the breadcrumbs in the milk for 15-20 minutes. Cook the zucchini in boiling water for 5 minutes. Drain and cool. Slice them in half lengthways and scoop out the flesh, leaving a thick shell at least ¼ inch. Take care not to break or crack the zucchini. Keep the scooped flesh on one side. Squeeze out the excess milk from the breadcrumbs and put them into a bowl. Fry the scooped zucchini flesh, chopped onion, tomatoes,

This page: Eggplant Bake (top left), Okra Curry (center right) and Okra Fry (right).

Overleaf: Zucchini Bake (left), Stuffed Zucchini (center) and Spicy Corn (right).

mushrooms and chopped garlic in half the olive oil for 5 minutes. Mix with the breadcrumbs, oregano, salt and pepper to taste, the beaten egg and half the cheeses. Spoon the mixture evenly into all the zucchini shells. Arrange the stuffed zucchini on a lightly greased baking tray. Sprinkle the remaining cheese over them and brush with the rest of the oil. Bake for 18-20 minutes at 400°F or until the cheese has melted and turned golden brown. Serve at once.

Spicy Corn

This dish originates from East Africa, it makes a tasty hot snack or supper dish.

PREPARATION TIME: 15 minutes

COOKING TIME: 35-40 minutes

SERVES: 6 people

3¾ tblsp oil
1 large onion, peeled and chopped
2 medium potatoes, peeled and cubed
8 fresh Chinese parsley leaves (optional)
¾ tsp cumin seed
¾ tsp mustard seed
1¼ tsp crushed fresh root ginger
1¼ tsp crushed garlic
1½lb frozen sweetcorn kernels
1¼ tsp salt
1¼ tsp chili powder
1¼ tsp ground coriander
¾ tsp ground turmeric
15oz can peeled tomatoes, chopped
1¼ tblsp tomato paste
1-2 green chilies, chopped
2 green peppers, seeded and cut into 1 inch pieces
3 sprigs fresh green coriander, chopped
1¼ tblsp thick tamarind pulp, or
2½ tblsp lemon juice

Heat the oil and fry the onion for 3 minutes; add the potatoes and fry for 5 minutes. Add the Chinese parsley leaves, cumin and mustard seed and stir fry for 1-2 minutes. Add ginger and garlic and stir fry for 1-2 minutes. Add the sweetcorn, salt, chili powder, ground coriander and turmeric. Mix well and cook for 2-3 minutes. Add the chopped tomatoes, tomato paste, chopped chilies, green peppers and coriander leaves.

Stir in the tamarind pulp and mix well adding a little water if the mixture seems too dry. Cover and cook over a low heat until the potatoes are tender about 10-15 minutes. The spicy corn should be thick but moist. Serve hot or cold.

Spiced Peas

PREPARATION TIME: 10 minutes

COOKING TIME: 15 minutes

SERVES: 6 people

2 tblsp oil
1 large onion, peeled and chopped
2 green chilies, sliced in half lengthwise
2lb shelled peas (fresh or frozen)
Salt and freshly ground black pepper to taste
1 tblsp lemon juice
Lemon wedges

Heat the oil in a wok or solid based frying pan and fry the onion until tender. Add the chilies and fry for 1 minute. Add the peas and salt and pepper to taste; stir fry for 5-10 minutes, or until well colored and "dry". Put into a serving dish and sprinkle with lemon juice. Garnish with lemon wedges. Serve as a side dish, or as a snack.

Spinach with Paneer

Paneer is a home-made cheese; it is made by separating milk into curds and whey by means of a souring agent such as lemon juice. It is eaten extensively in northern parts of India and is a good source of protein.

PREPARATION TIME: 15 minutes, plus time for making paneer

COOKING TIME: 20-30 minutes

SERVES: 4 people

To make paneer: (This is an overnight process)
2½ pints milk
2 tblsp lemon juice

Bring the milk to the boil. Reduce the heat and sprinkle with the lemon juice. The milk will separate into pale, watery whey and thick, white paneer (or curds). Remove from the heat and allow the paneer to coagulate (if the milk has not separated properly, add a few more

drops of lemon juice. The whey should be a clear, pale, yellow liquid. Pour the paneer and liquid through a muslin-lined sieve. Discard the liquid whey and tie the muslin over the paneer. Flatten the paneer to ½ inch thick; place it on a tray and rest it in a tilted position. Place more muslin over the top and weight it down. The pressure will drag out the remaining moisture and the tilted position will channel the liquid away from the paneer. Leave to drain overnight. Next day, cut the firm paneer into 1 inch cubes.

6 tblsp butter
1 medium onion, peeled and finely chopped
1 inch piece cinnamon stick
1 bayleaf
1lb frozen spinach paste, or fresh leaf spinach, cooked and pureed
1 tsp chili powder
½ tsp salt
½ cup natural yogurt
3 sprigs fresh green coriander leaves, chopped
1 tsp garam masala powder (hot, aromatic powder)
Oil for deep frying

Heat the butter in a pan and fry the onion until golden brown. Add the cinnamon and bayleaf and fry for 1 minute. Add the spinach and stir to mix. Sprinkle with the chili powder and salt and stir in the yogurt, coriander leaves and garam masala. Cover and cook for 2-3 minutes. Simmer gently. Meanwhile, deep-fry the drained paneer cubes until golden. Add the paneer cubes to the spinach and simmer together for 4-5 minutes. Serve hot with chapati or pulao rice.

New Potato Fry

This Oriental dish is very versatile; it can be served as a side dish, as a snack, or as a main curry. It is also a wonderful way of serving potatoes with traditional roast meats.

PREPARATION TIME: 20 minutes

COOKING TIME: 10-12 minutes

SERVES: 3-4 people

3 tblsp oil
1 tsp mustard seed
1lb small, even sized new potatoes, boiled in their skins and peeled
1 tsp red chili powder

1½ tsp ground coriander
¼ tsp ground turmeric
½ tsp salt
3 sprigs fresh green coriander leaves chopped (optional)
Lemon juice to taste

Heat the oil in a wok or solid based frying pan and add the mustard seed and the whole, peeled potatoes. Stir fry over a low heat until they are lightly browned. Sprinkle with the spices, salt and chopped coriander leaves. Stir over a low heat for 5-6 minutes until golden brown. Remove from heat. Put into a dish and sprinkle with the lemon juice. Serve hot or cold.

Zucchini Bake

Serve this dish as a main course with fried rice, or as a side dish.

PREPARATION TIME: 20-30 minutes

COOKING TIME: 35 minutes

SERVES: 4-6 people

2lbs zucchini trimmed and coarsely grated
1¼ tsp salt
2½ tblsp melted unsalted butter (or oil)
3-4 eggs, well beaten
1½-1¾ cups grated mild cheese (Edam, Samso, etc)
1 medium onion, peeled and finely chopped
2 cloves garlic, peeled and finely chopped
2½ tblsp chopped parsley
1¼ tsp dried basil
¾ tsp freshly ground black pepper
¼-⅓ cup grated Parmesan cheese

Put the grated zucchini into a colander and sprinkle with salt. Leave to drain for 10 minutes. Squeeze the moisture out of the zucchini until quite dry. Lightly grease a baking dish (size approx

Facing page: Spiced Peas (top), Spinach with Paneer (center right) and New Potato Fry (bottom).

x 7 inches). Heat the butter in a non-stick frying pan and fry the zucchini for 3-4 minutes until tender. Mix the beaten eggs, grated cheese, chopped onion, garlic, parsley, basil and pepper. Place the sauteed zucchini in the baking dish and pour egg mixture over the top. Sprinkle with the Parmesan cheese and bake at 350°F for 25-30 minutes until set. Serve cut into squares or diamond shapes. Can be eaten hot or cold.

Vegetable Stir Fry with Tofu (Soybean Curd)

This is a Chinese stir fry dish with soybean curd which makes a filling main course.

PREPARATION TIME: 30 minutes

COOKING TIME: 10 minutes

SERVES: 4 people

2½ tsp soya sauce
2½ tsp Worcestershire sauce
1 inch fresh root ginger, peeled and thinly sliced
3 cloves garlic, peeled and crushed
½lb Soybean Curd, cut into ½inch pieces
2½ tsp cornstarch
1 cup water
3¾ tblsp oil
3 stalks celery, sliced thinly
2 carrots, peeled and cut into thin diagonal slices
2-3 zucchini, trimmed, and cut into thin diagonal slices
1 green pepper, quartered, seeded and sliced thinly
8 mushrooms, thinly sliced
1-2 tomatoes, cut into wedges
½ cup snow peas, or thinly sliced green beans

Mix the soya sauce with the Worcestershire sauce, ginger and garlic. Add the soybean curd cubes and marinate for 8 minutes. Pick out the soybean curd and keep on a plate. Stir the cornstarch into the soya sauce mixture and blend in the water. Heat the oil in a wok over a medium heat. Add the celery and carrots and stir fry for 2 minutes. Add the zucchini and green pepper and stir fry for 2 minutes. Add the tomatoes and snow peas or green beans. Stir fry for 2 minutes. Add the mushrooms and stir fry for 1 minute. Stir in the water and soya sauce mixture. Cook until thickened, stirring for

1-2 minutes. Add the soybean curd. Heat through and serve immediately.

Cheese Bourag

PREPARATION TIME: 30-40 minutes

COOKING TIME: 20-25 minutes

SERVES: 4 people

2 cups flour
Salt
4 tsp baking powder
3 tblsp unsalted butter
½-⅔ cup milk
2 cups strong Cheddar cheese, grated
3 tblsp chopped parsley
Oil for deep frying

Sieve the flour, ¼ tsp salt and baking powder into a bowl; rub in the butter. Add the milk, a little at a time, and mix to a dough with a palette knife. Cover the dough and leave in a cool place to relax. Mix the grated cheese with the chopped parsley and a little salt to taste. Roll the dough out very thinly on a floured board and cut into 2 inch squares. Brush the edges of half the squares with a dampened pastry brush. Place a little filling in the centre of each one and cover with the remaining squares. Seal the edges well by pinching with the fingers or notching with the prongs of a fork. Heat the oil for deep frying. Fry the bourags a few at a time in hot oil until golden and crisp. Drain on kitchen paper and serve hot with sweet and sour sauce.

Avial

This is a mixed vegetable dish made with coconut.

PREPARATION TIME: 30 minutes

COOKING TIME: 20 minutes

SERVES: 4 people

2 medium sized potatoes, peeled and cut into 1 inch cubes
1½ cups lobia beans, trimmed and cut into 2 inch pieces
½ cup green beans, trimmed and sliced
4 drumstick or yard long beans, strung and cut into 1 inch pieces
1½ cups squash, peeled and cut into 1 inch cubes
1 green unripe banana, peeled and cut into 1 inch pieces

1 eggplant, trimmed and cut into 1 inch chunks
1 cup shelled peas
½ fresh coconut, shelled, skin removed and thinly sliced
1½ tsp cumin seeds
2 green chilies, chopped
½ cup water
⅔ cup natural yogurt
3 tblsp coconut oil for cooking

Steam all the vegetables for 10-15 minutes until almost tender, but still slightly crisp. Grind the spices with the water in a liquidizer until smooth. Mix the spice liquid with the coconut. Heat the coconut oil in a saucepan and add the vegetables, spice mixture and yogurt. Bring to the boil and simmer with the lid on for 5 minutes. Serve with rice.

Garlic Hash Brown

This is a favorite American dish eaten with steak and burgers.

PREPARATION TIME: 20 minutes

COOKING TIME: 30 minutes

SERVES: 4 people

5 tblsp oil
4 cloves of garlic, peeled and quartered lengthwise
3 whole red chilies
Salt
1-1½lb potatoes, peeled and coarsely grated

Heat the oil in a wok or a large non-stick frying pan. Fry the garlic until lightly browned. Add the red chilies and fry for 30 seconds. Sprinkle with salt to taste and add the grated potato. Stir fry for 5 minutes. Cover and cook for a further 8-10 minutes. The potatoes should be crisp and golden brown. Cook until the potatoes are tender. Serve as a side dish or for breakfast.

Vegetable Stir Fry with Tofu (top), Avial (center left) and Cheese Bourag (bottom right).

Spiced Chick Peas

This dryish curry is a "must" on any Punjabi menu. It is usually served with milk bread or pitta bread and an onion salad.

PREPARATION TIME: overnight for soaking, plus 15 minutes

COOKING TIME: 40-50 minutes

SERVES: 4-6 people

1lb chick peas
1 tsp baking powder
4 cloves
1 tsp cumin seed
4 large black cardamoms, ground
4 small cardamoms, ground
1 large onion, peeled and chopped
3 tblsp oil
2 bayleaves
1 inch piece cinnamon stick
2 green chilies, sliced in half
    lengthwise
1 inch fresh root ginger, peeled and
    finely chopped
4 cloves garlic, peeled and crushed
1½ tsp ground coriander
1-1¼ cups canned tomatoes, chopped
½ tsp freshly ground black pepper
½ tsp salt
5-6 sprigs fresh green coriander
    leaves, chopped

Wash the chick peas and soak them overnight in 2½ pints water and the baking powder. The following day, cook the chick peas in their soaking liquid in a pressure cooker for 10-15 minutes. If a lot of liquid has been absorbed during soaking, add a little more. Dry roast the cloves and cumin seed in a frying pan. Grind the cloves, cumin, large and small cardamons into a fine powder. Fry the onion in the oil for 2-3 minutes. Add the bayleaves, cinnamon, chilies, ginger and garlic. Fry for 1 minute, add the ground coriander and tomatoes. Fry for 2-3 minutes. Strain the chick peas, retaining any liquid. Add the chick peas to the tomato mixture and add black pepper, salt and the dry roasted spices. Mix well and add 1 cup of the strained chick pea liquid. Sprinkle with chopped coriander; cover and cook for 8-10 minutes. Add a little extra liquid if necessary. Serve with bread or rice.

Vegetable Pancakes (far left) and Spiced Chick Peas (left).

Vegetable Pancakes

A combination of shredded vegetables makes a delicious pancake, when added to the batter before cooking.

PREPARATION TIME: 15 minutes

COOKING TIME: 15 minutes

SERVES: 4-6 people

A stick of butter
2 cups shredded or coarsely grated
  carrots
2 cups shredded or coarsely grated
  zucchini
4 cups shredded or coarsely grated
  potatoes
1 medium onion, thinly sliced
3 eggs, well beaten
1 cup soured cream
5 tblsp cornstarch
¾ tsp salt
¾ tsp freshly ground black pepper
Oil for frying
Wedges of lemon

Melt the butter in a frying pan; add the carrots, zucchini, potatoes and onion. Saute for 3-4 minutes, stirring continuously. Beat the eggs together with the soured cream, cornstarch and salt and pepper. Mix well. Stir in the semi-cooked vegetables. Mix together gently. Heat a large non-stick frying pan and brush with 2½ tsp oil; add 1¼ tblsp batter. Cook until light brown; turn the small pancake over and cook until the other side is also brown. Make 3 or 4 at a time. The size of the pancakes can be increased by using more batter for each pancake. Serve with salads or with tomato sauce as a light meal or snack.

Green Beans with Coconut

PREPARATION TIME: 10 minutes

COOKING TIME: 20 minutes

SERVES: 3-4 people

2½ tblsp oil
2 cloves garlic, peeled and crushed
2 green or red dried chilies
1lb green beans, sliced
½ tsp salt
2½ tblsp desiccated coconut, or
  grated fresh coconut

Heat the oil in a wok or frying pan. Add the garlic and fry until golden brown. Add the chilies and stir fry for 30 seconds. Add the green

beans and sprinkle with salt. Stir fry for 8-10 minutes until the beans are tender but still crisp. Sprinkle with the coconut and stir fry for a further 2-3 minutes. Serve as a side dish.

Mixed Vegetable Raita

Raitas are yogurt-based Indian dishes served as accompaniments to curries etc. Natural yogurt is usually mixed with fruits, vegetables, and herbs such as coriander or mint.

PREPARATION TIME: 10 minutes

SERVES: 4-6 people

1¼ cups natural yogurt
½ cucumber, chopped
1 small onion, peeled and chopped
2 tomatoes, chopped
2 stalks celery, chopped
1 small apple, cored and chopped
2 boiled potatoes, peeled and
  chopped
¼ tsp salt
¼ tsp freshly ground black pepper
1 sprig fresh green coriander, chopped

Beat the yogurt in a bowl. Add all the remaining ingredients, seasoning well with salt and pepper. Chill before serving.

Cannelloni with Spinach and Ricotta

PREPARATION TIME: 20 minutes

COOKING TIME: 1 hour
                          20 minutes

SERVES: 4 people

2½ tblsp olive oil or melted butter
1 large onion, peeled and finely
  chopped
2 large cloves garlic, peeled and
  crushed
15oz can peeled tomatoes, chopped
1¼ tblsp tomato paste
Salt and freshly ground black pepper
  to taste
1¾ tsp dried basil
¾ tsp dried oregano
¾lb cannelloni tubes
5 tblsp thick spinach puree
½lb Ricotta cheese
2½ tblsp grated Parmesan cheese

To make the sauce: heat the oil or butter and fry the onion and garlic for 2-3 minutes. Add the tomatoes and tomato paste and mix well.

Simmer for 2 minutes. Add the salt and pepper, basil and oregano. Cover and simmer for 10-15 minutes until thick.

Bring a large pan of salted water to the boil; cook the cannelloni tubes for 10 minutes until just tender. Do not overboil. Lift out the cannelloni tubes and put them into a bowl of cold water to cool quickly. Drain well. Mix together the spinach, ricotta and salt and pepper to taste. Fill the cannelloni tubes with the spinach mixture and arrange them in a greased shallow ovenproof dish. Pour the tomato sauce over the cannelloni; sprinkle with the Parmesan cheese. Bake for 20-30 minutes at 350°F or until the top is brownd and bubbling. Serve at once.

Ginger Cauliflower

This is a very simple and extremely subtle vegetable dish spiced with ginger.

PREPARATION TIME: 15 minutes

COOKING TIME: 15 minutes

SERVES: 4 people

4 tblsp oil
1 medium onion, peeled and chopped
1 inch fresh root ginger, peeled and
  sliced
1-2 green chilies, cut in half
  lengthwise
1 medium cauliflower, cut into 1 inch
  flowerets, along with tender leaves
  and stalk
Salt to taste
2-3 sprigs fresh green coriander
  leaves, chopped
Juice of 1 lemon

Heat the oil in a wok or solid based saucepan; fry the onion, ginger and chilies for 2-3 minutes. Add the cauliflower and salt to taste. Stir to mix well. Cover and cook over a low heat for 5-6 minutes. Add the coriander leaves and cook for a further 2-3 minutes, or until the flowerets of cauliflower are tender. Sprinkle with lemon juice, mix well and serve immediately. Serve with pitta bread.

Noodles with Vegetables (top left), Green Beans with Coconut (center right) and Garlic Hash Brown (bottom).

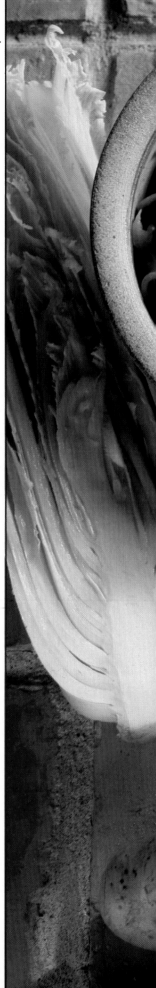

Mung Fritters

These tiny marble-sized fritters are made with mung pulse. They can be eaten as a cocktail snack or made into a curry with a well-flavored sauce.

PREPARATION TIME:	1 hour 30 minutes
COOKING TIME:	30 minutes
SERVES:	4 people

2 cups split mung pulse
1 small onion, peeled and chopped
1 tsp chili powder
1½ tsp garam masala powder (hot aromatic powder)
½ tsp cumin seed
4-5 sprigs fresh green coriander leaves, chopped
½ tsp salt
Oil for deep frying

Wash and soak the mung pulse for 1 hour in sufficient cold water to cover. Drain and then grind into a thick, coarse paste, adding ½-1 cup water as you go. It should be the consistency of peanut butter. Mix the mung paste with the onion, chili powder, garam masala, cumin seed, coriander leaves and salt. Mix well and adjust seasoning if necessary. Heat the oil for deep frying. Using a teaspoon, shape the paste into small "marbles" and fry in the hot oil until golden brown. Drain on kitchen paper and serve piping hot with chutney, a chili sauce or a dip. To turn into a curry, add the Mung Fritters to the following curry sauce.

Sauce
2 tsp oil
1 small onion, finely chopped
½ tsp chili powder
1 tsp ground coriander
1 tsp ground cumin
4-6 canned tomatoes, chopped
Salt to taste
3-4 sprigs fresh green coriander leaves, chopped

Heat the oil in a saucepan and fry the onion for 3 minutes. Stir in all the above ingredients; cover and simmer for 5-8 minutes. Add a little water to make a thickish sauce. Add ready-fried Mung Fritters and simmer for 3-5 minutes.

Noodles with Vegetables

This exotic noodle dish can be served hot or cold, as a main course, as a side dish or as a snack.

PREPARATION TIME:	20 minutes
COOKING TIME:	30 minutes
SERVES:	4 people

Salt to taste
1lb egg noodles, or broken spaghetti
3¾ tblsp oil
1 inch fresh root ginger, peeled and thinly sliced
1 large or 2 medium onions, peeled and sliced
⅔ cup green beans, sliced
⅔ cup carrots, peeled and cut into matchstick strips
1 cup white cabbage, or Chinese leaves, shredded
½ cup shelled peas
⅔ cup sprouting mung beans
1 green pepper, seeded and cut into 1 inch pieces
1-2 stalks celery, chopped
1-2 green chilies, split lengthways
¾ tsp monosodium glutamate (optional)
2½ tblsp soya sauce
1¼ tblsp lemon juice
1¼-2½ tsp Chinese red pepper sauce
5 tblsp chicken stock

Bring a large pan of water to the boil and add 1¼ tsp salt. Add the noodles or spaghetti and boil gently for 5-6 minutes. Drain the noodles. Rinse the noodles in cold water and drain once again. Heat the oil in a wok or large frying pan. Fry the ginger for 1-2 minutes. Add the onions and fry for 2-3 minutes. Add the beans and carrots and fry for 2 minutes. Add the remaining vegetables and the chilies and stir fry for 3-4 minutes. Add salt to taste and the noodles. Stir lightly with two forks. Dissolve the monosodium glutamate in the soya sauce and sprinkle over the noodle mixture; stir in the lemon juice, Chinese sauce and stock. Heat through for 2-3 minutes. Serve ▶

This page: Mung Fritters.

Facing page: Ginger Cauliflower (top left), Mixed Vegetable Raita (top right) and Cannelloni with Spinach and Ricotta (bottom).

Sauces, Dips and Chutney

Plum Chutney

Any variety of plum can be used; either singly or in a mixture of one or more varieties.

PREPARATION TIME: 10 minutes

COOKING TIME: 40 minutes

MAKES: about 6lbs

4½lb plums, pitted
1 inch fresh root ginger, peeled and finely chopped
2 tsp salt
3lb brown sugar
1 tsp cumin seed
1 tsp coriander seed
4 dried red chilies
1 tsp onion seed
2½ tblsp cider vinegar
½ cup chopped blanched almonds
½ cup chopped cashew nuts or hazelnuts
1 cup raisins
1 cup white raisins

Put the plums, ginger, salt and sugar into a saucepan, preferably a non-stick pan. Cover and cook gently until the plums are soft (about 15-20 minutes). Dry roast the cumin seed, coriander seed and red chilies in a frying pan for 1-2 minutes. Remove the red chilies and coarsely grind the cumin and coriander seeds. Add the roasted red chilies, ground spices and onion seed to the cooked plums. Add the cider vinegar, nuts, raisins and white raisins and simmer gently for 5-6 minutes. Allow to cool slightly. Pour into clean, warm glass jars and seal.

Guacamole
(AVOCADO DIP)

This is a popular Mexican dip, usually eaten with crisps, salty biscuits or sticks of raw vegetable, such as cucumber, celery etc.

PREPARATION TIME: 5 minutes

SERVES: 6-8 people

1 avocado, peeled, stoned and mashed
1 large clove garlic, peeled and crushed
1 tsp salt
¼ tsp freshly ground black pepper
1 large tomato, skinned and chopped
1 tsp olive oil
1 tblsp lemon juice
2-3 sprigs fresh green coriander leaves, finely chopped
1 small onion, peeled and grated

Blend the avocado pulp in the liquidizer with the salt, pepper, tomato, olive oil, lemon juice and coriander leaves. Put into a small bowl and mix with the onion. Serve with savory biscuits, crisps or sticks of raw vegetables.

Tamarind Dip

PREPARATION TIME: 20 minutes

MAKES: about 1½ cups

¾ cup tamarind pods
1 cup boiling water
½ tsp salt
7 tblsp brown sugar
1 green chili, chopped
¼ tsp chili powder

Soak the tamarind pods in boiling water for 5-6 minutes, or until soft. Rub the pods in the water to separate the dried pulp around the seeds. Squeeze out the seeds and skins of the pods. (Do not discard as a second extract can be obtained for future use.) Add the salt and sugar to the tamarind pulp. Mix in the chili and chili powder and leave to stand for 5 minutes before using. Salt and sugar can be adjusted according to personal taste.

Savory Coconut Chutney

PREPARATION TIME: 15 minutes

MAKES: about 1¾ cups

1-2 fresh coconuts, shell removed, outer skin peeled and cut into pieces
½ inch fresh root ginger, peeled and chopped
2 green chilies, chopped
1 tsp cumin seed
1-2 bunches fresh green coriander leaves, chopped
4 tblsp thick tamarind pulp or
5 tblsp lemon juice
1 tsp sugar
½ tsp salt

Put all the ingredients into the liquidizer and blend until smooth and creamy. If the mixture is too thick, add a little water. Serve with hot snacks, such as toasted chicken sandwiches.

Mixed Fruit Chutney

This sweet-sour chutney goes particularly well with pork dishes such as spareribs.

PREPARATION TIME: 30 minutes

COOKING TIME: 40 minutes

MAKES: about 5¼lb

3 firm pears, cored and sliced
4 apples, cored and chopped
4 peaches, skinned, stoned and sliced or
15oz can peach slices, drained
1lb plums, halved and stoned
6 rings canned pineapple, cut into cubes
1 cup dates, stoned and chopped
2 cups dried prunes, soaked overnight
1 cup dried apricots, soaked overnight
2¼lb brown sugar
2 tsp salt
1 inch fresh root ginger, peeled and thinly sliced
1 cup chopped blanched almonds
1 cup cashew nuts, chopped
5 tblsp cider vinegar
8 cloves, coarsely ground
1 tsp chili powder
2 inch piece cinnamon stick
2 bananas, peeled and sliced

Put all the fruit into a saucepan (apart from the bananas) with the sugar, salt and ginger. Cover and cook for 15-20 minutes. Add the nuts, vinegar, cloves, chili powder and cinnamon stick. Stir well and cook for 6-8 minutes. Simmer gently, stirring occasionally, until most of the liquid has evaporated. The chutney should be thick and sticky. Add the sliced bananas and stir over the heat for 1 minute. Cool slightly. Pour into clean, warm glass jars and seal.

Green Tomato Relish

Use the last crop of tomatoes make this relish. Serve with a grilled meat, barbecued chick etc.

PREPARATION TIME: 4 hou

COOKING TIME: about 20 minute

MAKES: about 3lb

2lb green tomatoes, seeded and chopped
1½ cups shredded white cabba
2 red peppers, seeded and chop
1 onion, peeled and chopped
1¼ tblsp salt
1 cup brown sugar
1¼ cups distilled white vinegar
2 tsp mustard seed
2 tsp celery seed
1½ tblsp prepared horseradish

Mix the tomatoes, cabbage, peppers and onion together. Sprinkle with the salt and mi Leave to stand for 2-3 hours well and then rinse under co running water. Drain and ger squeeze out the excess moist Mix the sugar, vinegar, musta seed, celery seed and horsera sauce together in a large solic based pan. Bring to the boil medium heat. Add the veget cover and simmer gently for another 16-18 minutes until t relish is sticky. Remove from heat and cool slightly. Pour ir clean, warm glass jars and sea keep for up to 2 months.

Facing page: Plum Chutne (top right), Mixed Fruit Chutney (center) and Gre Tomato Relish (bottom).

**Tamarind Dip (far left),
Savory Coconut Chutney
(center) and Guacamole
(Avocado Dip) (above).**

little olive oil or chicken stock.

Chili Sauce

This classic piquant sauce is pe[rfect] for those who love hot, spicy f[ood].

| PREPARATION TIME: 20 min |
| COOKING TIME: 2 hours 30 minutes |
| MAKES: about 600ml (1 pint) |

8 large ripe tomatoes, skinned a[nd] chopped
2-3 small green peppers, seeded [and] chopped
2 medium onions, peeled and fi[nely] chopped
4 stalks celery, chopped
3 tsp salt
1 cup + 2 tblsp granulated suga[r]
1½ cups cider vinegar
2-3 bay leaves
1 tsp coriander seeds
1 tsp freshly ground black peppe[r]
¼ tsp ground cloves
½ tsp ground cinnamon
1 tsp ground ginger
1 tsp mustard seed

Mix all the ingredients togethe[r in] a pan and bring to the boil. C[over] and simmer for about 2 hours [on] a low heat, until thick. Stir on[ce,] mix and simmer again for 10 minutes. Remove from the he[at] and cool slightly. Pour into cle[an,] warm glass jars and seal.

Mexican Salsa

This is a beautiful fresh sauce which goes well with barbecued meats, curries and, of course, burritos and tacos.

| PREPARATION TIME: 10 minutes |
| MAKES: about ⅔ cup |

5 tomatoes, skinned and chopped
1 small onion, chopped
1-2 pickled or canned Mexican chilies, chopped
2 cloves garlic, peeled and crushed
2 tsp cider vinegar
½ tsp salt
½ tsp sugar
2-3 sprigs fresh green coriander, chopped
1 tsp bottled chili sauce

Mix all the ingredients together in a bowl. Chill for 2 to 3 hours before serving.

Salsa Verde

A perfect Italian sauce to serve with any pasta, or with veal.

| PREPARATION TIME: 15 minutes |
| MAKES: about 1 cup |

6 tblsp chopped fresh parsley
2½ tblsp white wine vinegar
3 cloves garlic, peeled and sliced
2 tblsp capers, finely chopped
2 tblsp olive oil
2-3 scallions, chopped
Salt and freshly ground black pepper to taste

Blend the parsley, garlic and vinegar in the liquidizer. Pour the parsley sauce into a small bowl and mix with the capers, olive oil, scallions and salt and pepper. Mix well. Cover and chill for 10-15 minutes. The sauce can be thinned to the desired consistency with a

This page: **Chili Sauce (top left), Salsa Verdi (center) an[d] Mexican Salsa (bottom).**

Facing page: **Rice Pudding (top), Potato Pudding (cent[er] and Cabbage Pudding (bottom).**

Sweets

Carrotella

PREPARATION TIME: 15 minutes

COOKING TIME: 35-40 minutes

SERVES: 4-6 people

2½ pints milk
1lb carrots, peeled and shredded
1 cup canned evaporated milk
½ cup granulated sugar
½ cup raisins
Seeds of 8 small cardamoms, crushed
2 drops rose-water or vanilla essence
½ cup chopped blanched almonds
½ cup pistachio nuts, chopped

Put the milk into a pan and simmer over a low heat until reduced to 2 pints. Add the carrots; cover and cook over a medium heat for 15 minutes. Add the evaporated milk, sugar and raisins. Cover and simmer gently for another 5 minutes. Remove from the heat. Stir in the crushed cardamom seeds and essence and pour into a serving dish. Allow to cool slightly. Sprinkle nuts on the top and serve. On hot summer days, the Carrotella is best chilled.

Carrot Cake

PREPARATION TIME: 30 minutes

COOKING TIME: 45-50 minutes

MAKES: 10 inch loaf

¾ cup butter
¾ cup brown sugar
½ cup granulated sugar
2 eggs, well beaten
2 cups flour
1½ tsp bicarbonate of soda
½ tsp baking powder
¼ tsp ground cinnamon
½ tsp salt
2 cups peeled carrots, shredded
¾ cup raisins
½ cup chopped walnuts
¼ tsp small cardamom seeds, crushed
Confectioner's sugar for dredging

Cream the butter and sugars together. Add the eggs, a little at a time, beating well after each addition. Sieve the flour, bicarbonate of soda, baking powder, cinnamon and salt

together. Fold the dry ingredients into the egg mixture. Add the carrots, raisins, nuts and crushed cardamom. Mix well and pour the mixture into a well buttered 10 inch loaf tin. Bake at 350°F for 45-50 minutes, or until a fine metal skewer comes out clean when inserted into the centre of the cake. Cool in the tin for 10-15 minutes, before turning out. Dredge with Confectioner's sugar before serving.

Rice Pudding

There are many ways of making a rice pudding, but this is definitely one of the best. It is suitable for serving on any occasion, from everyday meals to smart dinner parties.

PREPARATION TIME: 10 minutes

COOKING TIME: 1 hour 30 minutes

SERVES: 6 people

¼ cup unsalted butter
1 bayleaf, crumbled
1 inch piece cinnamon stick, crushed
1½ cups pudding rice, washed and drained
2½ pints milk
1½ cups canned evaporated milk
¾ cup granulated sugar
½ cup raisins
½ cup chopped blanched almonds
½ cup pistachio nuts, chopped or cut into slivers
Seeds of 8 small cardamoms, crushed

Melt the butter in a saucepan and fry the bayleaf and cinnamon for 1 minute. Add the rice and stir well. Add the milk and bring to the boil. Reduce the heat and simmer for 40-50 minutes, stirring occasionally to prevent the rice from sticking to the pan. Add the sugar and evaporated milk, and simmer for a further 20-30 minutes, stirring frequently. Thin layers of light brown skin form on the base of the pan, this is what gives the pudding its rich reddish tinge and flavor. Add the raisins and half the chopped almonds. Mix well and simmer for a further 5-10 minutes,

or until the pudding is really thick. Mix in the crushed cardamom seeds and pour into a serving dish. Decorate with the remaining chopped almonds and pistachio nuts. Serve hot or cold.

Carrot Halva

A delightful sweet from the mysterious East. Serve it hot or cold, with or without cream.

PREPARATION TIME: 20 minutes

COOKING TIME: 50 minutes

SERVES: 8-10 people

4lb large sweet carrots, peeled and shredded
2 pints canned evaporated milk
3 cups granulated sugar
¾ cup unsalted butter
¾ cup raisins
Seeds of 10 small cardamoms, crushed
1 cup chopped mixed nuts (blanched and chopped almonds, cashews, pistachios etc.)
Light cream

Put the carrots, evaporated milk and sugar into a large, solid based pan and bring to the boil. Reduce the heat and cook the carrots gently for 30-40 minutes, or until the milk has evaporated. Add the butter and raisins and stir over a gentle heat for 8-10 minutes, until the Halva is dark and leaves the sides of the pan clean. Add the cardamom seeds and mix well. Pour into a flat shallow dish about 1 inch deep. Flatten the Halva evenly with a spatula. Sprinkle with the chopped nuts. Serve hot or cold, cut into squares, with light cream.

Potato Pudding

This old-fashioned Oriental pudding has a rich and lovely flavor. It keeps for weeks and can be frozen.

PREPARATION TIME: 15 minutes

COOKING TIME: 1 hour 15 minutes

SERVES: 6 people

2lb potatoes, peeled and shredde
1 cup unsalted butter
1½ pints canned evaporated mil
1½ cups granulated sugar
1 cup ground almonds
¼ tsp saffron
½ cup chopped almonds and pistachios

Wash the potatoes thoroughly drain them well. Squeeze the potatoes to remove all excess moisture. Put the potatoes, bu and evaporated milk into a larg solid based saucepan and cook slowly until mushy. The potato will disintegrate into a mashed state as they cook. Add the sug and stir to dissolve. The mixtu will bubble and splatter like bubbling mud from hot spring Wrap a damp tea towel aroun your hand and stir the mixture 20-30 minutes over a gentle he Add the ground almonds and saffron. Continue stirring over heat until the pudding become thick, sticky and oily on the surface. Pour the pudding into shallow dish and decorate with chopped nuts.

Cabbage Pudding

PREPARATION TIME: 10 minu

COOKING TIME: 40 minutes

SERVES: 4-6 people

1½ cups finely shredded white cabbage
2 tblsp pudding rice
2½ pints milk
1 cup canned evaporated milk
1 inch piece cinnamon stick
1 bayleaf
½-¾ cups granulated sugar
½ cup raisins

Facing page: Carrot Cake (top), Carrot Halva (center) and Carrotella (bottom).

½ cup chopped blanched almonds
½ cup pistachio nuts, chopped
Seeds of 6 small cardamoms, crushed

Put the cabbage, rice, both milks, cinnamon and bayleaf into a pan. Bring to the boil and simmer gently for 15-20 minutes, stirring occasionally to prevent the mixture from sticking to the pan. Add the sugar and simmer gently until the mixture is thick. Add the raisins and nuts. Remove from the heat when the rice is tender and the milk has been reduced to approx. 1¼ pints. Pour into a serving dish and sprinkle with the crushed cardamom seeds. Mix well and serve.

Frozen Lemon Yogurt Souffle

PREPARATION TIME: 20 minutes

SERVES: 4-6 people

2 pints natural yogurt
1 cup superfine sugar
Juice and finely grated rind of 2
    lemons
1 tsp vanilla essence
2 egg whites
¼ tsp salt
¼ tsp cream of tartar
½ cup heavy cream, whipped
Few thin lemon slices for decoration

Mix the yogurt, sugar, lemon juice, lemon rind and vanilla essence together. Whisk the egg whites, salt and cream of tartar until stiff but not dry. Fold the egg whites gently into the yogurt mixture, and then fold in the whipped cream. Pour the mixture into a souffle dish and freeze overnight. Garnish with lemon slices before serving. Serve either frozen or partially thawed.

Mango Fool

This delicious sweet can be made with fresh or canned mangoes; crushed cardamom seeds give it a characteristic flavor.

PREPARATION TIME: 10 minutes

SERVES: 4-6 people

1lb canned mango slices or the

equivalent amount of fresh mango, stoned and peeled
1 cup canned evaporated milk
Seeds of 6 cardamoms, crushed
Sugar to taste
Whipped cream

Put the mango, evaporated milk and cardamoms into a liquidizer and blend until smooth. Add a little sugar if necessary. Pour into a serving bowl and chill for 20 minutes before serving. Serve with whipped cream.

Tropical Fruit Dessert

An exotic sweet dish to finish any special meal. A delightful dessert from nature's fruit garden.

PREPARATION TIME: 30 minutes

SERVES: 8-10 people

4 bananas, cut into ¼ inch thick
    slices
5 rings pineapple, cut into chunks
    (fresh or canned)
2 semi-ripe pears, peeled, cored and
    cut into chunks
2 medium red-skinned apples, cored
    and cut into chunks
8 peach slices, chopped
2 cups red cherries, pitted
4 tblsp grated fresh coconut
1 honeydew melon, peeled and cut
    into chunks
1lb marshmallows
6-8 slices mango, cut into chunks
    (fresh or canned)
2 kiwi fruit, peeled and cut into
    chunks
20-25 strawberries, halved
Few seedless white and black grapes,
    halved
1½ tblsp confectioners' sugar
1 cup cottage cheese
Few drops vanilla essence

Mix all the ingredients together in a large bowl. Cover and chill for 1 hour.

Tropical Fruit Salad

This medley of fruits is very colorful and it offers a variety of tastes and textures.

PREPARATION TIME: 40 minutes

2 bananas, sliced
4 kiwi fruit, peeled and sliced
10 dates, stoned and sliced in half

2 guavas, halved and then sliced into
    wedges
1 pawpaw, cut into thin crescent
    shapes
1lb canned lychees, drained
8oz canned pineapple chunks,
    drained (or pieces of fresh
    pineapple)
2 fresh mangoes, peeled and sliced
Few seedless grapes, white and black,
    halved
1 small melon, cut into chunks
¼ water-melon, cut into chunks
4 fresh figs, halved

Dressing
2 tblsp lemon juice
Pinch salt
½ cup chopped toasted walnut or
    pine kernels

Prepare the fruits as suggested and arrange in a large glass bowl, in layers. Spoon over the lemon juice and sprinkle with salt. Sprinkle over the chopped nuts.

Semolina and Coconut Slices

PREPARATION TIME: 10 minutes

COOKING TIME: 30 minutes

SERVES: 6 people

¾ cup unsalted butter
1½ cups coarse semolina
2 cups shredded coconut
1½ cups granulated sugar
1 cup canned evaporated milk
1 cup water
1 cup chopped mixed nuts: blanched
    almonds, cashews, walnuts,
    hazelnuts and pistachios
¾ cup raisins
Seeds of 6 cardamoms, crushed

Melt the butter in a frying pan and add the semolina. Dry roast the semolina by stirring it until it turns lightly golden. Spoon onto a plate. Dry roast the coconut in the same pan until lightly golden. Add the

Tropical Fruit Dessert (top right), Frozen Lemon Yogurt Souffle (top left) and Tropical Fruit Salad (bottom).

semolina, sugar, milk and water to the coconut. Stir the mixture over the heat for 5-8 minutes. Add the chopped nuts, raisins and crushed cardamom seeds. Mix well and stir over a gentle heat for 5-6 minutes, until the mixture is thick and the oil begins to separate. Pour into a shallow dish, smooth with a spatula and allow to cool. Cut into diamond shapes or squares.

Mint Barley Sherbet

PREPARATION TIME: 10 minutes
COOKING TIME: 20 minutes
SERVES: 4-6 people

1 cup whole barley
2 pints water
¼ cup mint leaves, minced
Pinch salt

6 tblsp granulated sugar
Juice of 3 lemons
1-2 drops green food coloring
Grated rind of 1 lemon
Few mint leaves and lemon slices to decorate

Wash the barley in 2-3 changes of water. Soak the barley in the measured water for a few minutes; add the minced mint leaves and

This page: Yogurt, Almond and Saffron Sherbet (top center), Mango Sherbet (left) Maori Shake (center) and Tropical Blizzard (right).

Facing page: Mint Barley Sherbet (top left), Spiced Te (top right) and Rich Coffee (bottom).

bring to the boil. Simmer gently for 10-15 minutes. Remove from the heat and strain; discard the barley grains. Dissolve the salt and sugar in the barley liquid; add the lemon juice, colouring and lemon rind. Mix well and make up to 2 pints with water. Pour into glasses and add crushed ice. To make clear sherbet; allow the barley water to stand for 10 minutes, so that the starch settles. Pour off the clear liquid and serve with a twist of lemon and mint leaves floating on the top.

Yogurt Dessert

This yogurt dessert is a light, delicious way of ending a rich meal; it is also simple and easy to make.

PREPARATION TIME: 15 minutes, plus setting time

COOKING TIME: 15 minutes

SERVES: 4-6 people

3 quarts milk
8-10 tblsp granulated sugar or to taste
½ cup finely chopped blanched almonds
½ cup raisins
Seeds of 8 small cardamoms, crushed
2-3 drops rose water or vanilla essence
2½ tblsp natural yogurt
¼ cup pistachio nuts, chopped

Simmer the milk in a large pan until it is reduced by half. Add the sugar to the milk and stir until dissolved. Add half the almonds, the raisins and cardamom seeds. Allow to cool until the milk is just tepid. Add the essence and beaten yogurt to the milk and stir well. Pour into a large, shallow serving dish. Cover and leave in a warm place, such as an airing cupboard, until the yogurt has set (about 5-6 hours). Sprinkle with the chopped pistachio nuts and remaining chopped almonds. Chill for 1 hour before serving. Will keep for up to 15 days in the refrigerator.

Tropical Blizzard

PREPARATION TIME: 3-4 minutes

SERVES: 4 people

1 cup pineapple juice or orange juice
1¼ cups natural yogurt
6 slices mango (canned or fresh)
1 tblsp sugar
Soda water
Ice cubes

Put the fruit juice, yogurt, mango and sugar into the liquidizer; blend for ½ minute. Pour into 4 glasses and dilute with soda water. Serve with ice cubes.

Maori Shake

A new taste experience; kiwi fruit blended with lemon yogurt.

PREPARATION TIME: 5 minutes

SERVES: 4-6 people

1 cup pineapple juice
2 kiwi fruits, peeled and chopped
1¼ cups lemon yogurt
Ice cubes
Lemonade
1 kiwi fruit, peeled and thinly sliced for decoration

Put the pineapple juice, chopped kiwi fruit and lemon yogurt into the liquidizer; blend for 30 seconds-1 minute, until smooth. Pour into 4-6 tall glasses; add ice cubes and top up with lemonade. Stir to mix. Serve with slices of kiwi fruit on top.

Mango Sherbet

This is a pretty green mango sherbet made from unripe mangoes. Windfallen mangoes are usually used for making this refreshing drink in India.

PREPARATION TIME: 20 minutes

COOKING TIME: 5-6 minutes

SERVES: 6 people

2 medium size unripe mangoes
⅓ tsp salt
2¼ pints water
Sugar to taste
Crushed ice

Boil the mangoes in sufficient water to cover for 5-6 minutes. Remove and allow to cool under cold running water. Peel off the skins. Put the water and salt into a punch bowl. Scrape all the mango flesh away from the stones and add to the punch bowl. Discard the stones. Whisk the sherbet until well blended. Pour into tall glasses; add sugar to taste and crushed ice.

Yogurt, Almond and Saffron Sherbet

A good healthy drink, which can be given a sweet or salty flavor.

PREPARATION TIME: 5 minutes

SERVES: 5-6 people

2¼ pints water
1 pint natural yogurt
2 tsp lemon juice
12 blanched almonds
¼ tsp saffron
2 drops vanilla essence or rose water
Salt or sugar to taste

Put 1½ cups water into the liquidizer with the yogurt, lemon juice, almonds, saffron and essence; blend until smooth. Mix in the remaining water. Pour into tall glasses over crushed ice. To make sweet sherbet, stir 2-3 tsp sugar into each glass; and to make a salty sherbet, sprinkle on a pinch of salt.

Rich Coffee

This is an old and traditional method of making coffee from the Orient.

PREPARATION TIME: 8 minutes

SERVES: 6-8 people

2¼ pints water
1 pint milk
2 tblsp freshly ground medium roast coffee
Seeds of 4 small cardamoms, crushed
Sugar to taste

Put the water and milk into a stainless steel pan and bring to the boil. Add the coffee and crushed cardamoms. Cover the pan and remove from the heat. Allow to brew for 2-3 minutes. Stir once. When the coffee grains settle to the bottom, strain off the coffee into cups and add sugar to taste.

Spiced Tea

This is a very different and interesting way of serving tea; it is refreshing served either hot or cold.

PREPARATION TIME: 5 minutes

SERVES: 6 people

2¼ pints water
1 pint milk
½ inch piece cinnamon stick
4 cloves
Seeds of 4 small cardamoms, crushed
6 teabags
or 2 tblsp tea leaves
Sugar to taste

Put the water, milk, cinnamon, cloves and cardamom seeds into a stainless steel pan. Bring to the boil and add the tea. Cover the pan and remove from the heat. Allow to brew for 2 minutes. Stir well. Add sugar to taste. Strain into cups and serve. Alternatively, allow the tea to cool and then chill and serve with ice.

Yogurt Dessert (top left), Mango Fool (left) and Semolina and Coconut Slices (bottom left).

Aloo Bonda 20
Avial 42
Banana and Nut Bread 32
Basic Pizza Dough 32
Bessan Omelettes 16
Cabbage Pudding 56
Cannelloni with Spinach and Ricotta 46
Carrot Cake 56
Carrot Halva 56
Carrot Soup 8
Carrotella 56
Cashew Nut Pie 18
Cheese Bourag 42
Cheese Salad 24
Cheese and Lentil Balls 18
Chili Sauce 54
Crusty Loaf 32
Cucumber Soup 8
Curry Puffs 15
Daal Soup 8
Dosas 13
Eggplant Bake 36
Flour Pancake 13
Fritters (Tempura) 18
Frozen Lemon Yogurt Souffle 58
Garlic Hash Brown 42
Ginger Cauliflower 46
Green Beans with Coconut 46
Green Tomato Relish 50
Guacamole (Avocado Dip) 50

Kedgeree 27
Mango Fool 58
Mango Sherbet 62
Maori Shake 62
Mexican Salsa 54
Minestrone Soup 10
Mint Barley Sherbet 60
Mixed Bean Salad 22
Mixed Daal 28
Mixed Fresh Vegetable Salad 25
Mixed Fruit Chutney 50
Mixed Nut Rissoles 18
Mixed Vegetable Pizza Topping 34
Mixed Vegetable Raita 46
Mixed Vegetable Soup 8
Mung Fritters 48
New Potato Fry 40
Noodles with Vegetables 48
Nutty Salad 22
Okra Curry 36
Okra Fry 36
Onion Salad 22
Onion Soup 12
Pakora 20
Paratha 31
Pasta Salad 26
Plum Chutney 50
Potato Cutlets 16
Potato Pudding 56
Puri 30
Quick Tomato Soup 11
Red Kidney Bean Curry 28
Red Lentil Daal 28
Rice and Mushroom Soup 12
Rice and Nut Salad 22
Rice Pudding 56

Rich Coffee 63
Roti 32
Salsa Verde 54
Samosa 15
Savory Coconut Chutney
Semolina and Coconut Slices 58
Spiced Chick Peas 45
Spiced Peas 40
Spiced Tea 63
Spicy Corn 40
Spinach with Paneer 40
Stuffed Squash 16
Stuffed Mushrooms 20
Stuffed Peppers 16
Stuffed Tomatoes 16
Stuffed Zucchini 36
Sweet and Sour Coleslaw 22
Sweet Savory Rice 28
Tabbouleh 22
Taco Pizza 34
Tamarind Dip 50
Tomati, Onion and Mushroom Flan 1
Tomato Saar 8
Tropical Blizzard 62
Tropical Fruit Dessert 58
Tropical Fruit Salad 58
Vegetable Kebabs 16
Vegetable Pancakes 46
Vegetable Pulao Rice 27
Vegetable Stir Fry with Tofu
    (Soybean Curd) 42
Whole-wheat Bread 32
Whole-wheat Pizza Dough 32
Yogurt, Almond and Saffron Sherbet
Yogurt Dessert 62
Zucchini Bake 40